Julie

Why oh Why?

Guide to the visible and invisible world

Contents

Why oh Why?
Guide to the visible and invisible world

is dedicated to my dear granddaughters

Eleonora & Amelia

Preface

This is the book that I wish had existed and that someone had given to me to read when I was younger. It has been written to help others realize that each and every one of us are truly divine essences and to indicate how to have a happier, richer life. It is the result of years of personal experiences, as well as knowledge gained from the works, studies and speeches conducted by spiritual teachers from the past and the present. I am deeply grateful to them all, who have so thoroughly answered my many questions pertaining to life, death and the afterworld. I have synthesized them here so that they can be accessed by many. A list of suggested books are indicated at the back of this book for those who want to further grasp the concepts and their significance.

PART 1
ABOUT PHYSICAL LIFE
ON PLANET EARTH

MAN, THE ELEMENTS, THE UNIVERSE AND ITS CREATOR

Is there chaos or order?
It is sometimes difficult for us to perceive the value of our daily contrasts, but there is a just and logical reason for everything. Man's thoughts and deeds fit into a divine plan that is in harmony with the Universe.

Who is our Creator?
There is only one Creator, though called with different names, such as God, Allah, He Who Is, Higher Source, Jehovah, Lord... Our Creator is an omniscient (all knowing), overwhelmingly powerful source of energy and pure unconditional love. He is eternal, the co-creator of all that is, that was and that will be, the deepest loving and thinking intelligence, as well as the highest vibrational energy existing in the Universe.

When did the Creator first come to be?
The Creator simply is and has always been. He is perennial energy, thought and love.

Where is the Creator?
Our Creator is omnipresent - present everywhere at the same time. He is also within every single one of us (We Are One). We are in fact divine beings though we may not be aware of this yet.

How were our spirits created?
Our Creator's love led to His contemplating and expanding Himself, through thought, thereby giving life to our spiritual essences, which are made of light.

3

He gave life simultaneously to every one of us, divine sparks of light. These divine essences, our spirits, are our original and eternal life forms. We are the Creator's manifested thought and we are forever inextricably a part of His divine intelligence. We are the beloved children of the Creator and gods in our own right.

Isn't it blasphemous to say that we are actually gods?

It's a tribute to our Creator for us to be able to recognize and acknowledge our divine, eternal essence. By embracing our true identity and realizing that we are powerful co-creators responsible for our lives, we deliberately give up our passive roles and take on the role of true protagonists. Indeed, if our hearts were truly open, we would be unlimited. Each of us would have the power to perform miracles as highly evolved spiritual beings, such as Jesus Christ and saints, have done and continue to do...

Who is man?

The human being is an energetic extension of the Creator. Man is a divine being existing in both the material and spiritual worlds. We are pure energy and light and we have been temporarily given a physical body so that we can have experiences on planet Earth and enjoy and learn from these.

What are the four parts of man?

The spirit, the soul, the mind and the physical body.

What is the spirit?

The spirit is an energetic extension of the Creator.

What is the soul?
Our soul is our true individual essence. This is Who We Really Are. It is the spiritual energy that stores and remembers everything that we feel, think, experience and learn. Our souls are intelligent consciousnesses temporarily hosted in physical bodies. Our soul memorizes our every thought and emotion and is that which distinguishes our personal identity from the other spirits/energetic extensions of the Creator.

What is the mind?
The mind is the mediator between the physical body and the soul. It has three facets: our *conscious mind*, which translates what we experience through our physical senses; our *unconscious mind*, which translates the information coming from our soul; and our *subconscious mind*, which is the link between the conscious and the unconscious mind.

When was the soul created?
Our souls were created after the Creator gave life to His energetic extensions, our individual spirits, so that we could each receive and interpret His love and store our individual emotions, our individual experiences, our individual memory.

When does the spirit (along with the soul) enter the physical body for the first time?
Spirits are free to enter the fetus at any time, though most enter for the first time between two to four months from conception. It's usually a gradual process though, with the spirit becoming increasingly present. Some spirits instead choose to go in and out of the fetus and also in and out of the child after it is born.

The spirit synchronizes with the child's brain, giving life to the mind, which is the mediator between the physical body and the soul.

When does the spirit (along with the soul) remain attached to the physical body?

When the child is between five and six years of age, the spirit usually remains attached to the child's physical body. Children gradually lose contact with the spiritual world when they are 5-6 years old.

Which changes occur in children when they are fully incarnated?

When children are between 5-6 years of age, the physical world becomes more and more important, while their awareness of the spiritual world slowly dissolves.

What are man's six senses?

Besides the five physical senses of sight, hearing, touch, smell and taste, man has a sixth sense called *intuition*. Intuitions arrive via your extrasensory perceptions and are the bridge between your conscious mind, which translates what you experience through your physical senses, and your unconscious mind, which translates the information coming from your soul.

Which are the extrasensory perceptions?

A. Clairvoyance (seeing with clarity)

This is when you see something in your mind (internally) or in your physical eyes (externally). You see images or scenes transmitted to you from the spiritual world.

The first time I started noticing that there was such a thing as clairvoyance was back in 1977. I was at some friends' house and it was very late at night. I wanted to go home but my boyfriend wasn't ready to go yet. I closed my eyes and "saw" a skull in my mind's eye. I thought: "Somebody is dead. I wonder who?" Soon after I went home and discovered that the kitten that I had recently found in the fields was lying on my shawl, dead.

B. Clairaudience (hearing with clarity)
This is when you hear something in your mind (internally) or in your physical ears (externally). You hear words, sounds or songs that are transmitted to you from the spiritual world.

In June 2017, before leaving for the U.S. to go see my Dad, I was worried since I had recently dreamt that the airplane I was traveling on had crashed into the ocean. So one night before sleep I asked my spirit guide if I'd still be alive for the day of my wedding anniversary a few weeks later and I heard this old song inside my head: "In Dublin's fair city, where girls are so pretty..." *It was the last words of the song that gave me the answer I was looking for:* "alive, alive-o"!

C. Clairsentience (feeling with clarity)
This is when you feel something in your mind (internally) or in your physical body (externally). You have gut instincts or feel physical sensations (pain, cold, excitement, dread...) that are transmitted to you from the spiritual world.

7

> *I was far from home when I clearly felt the sting of a needle on my thigh one night. On my return, my husband told me that our cat Atena had felt really bad and that he had brought her to the vet who had given her a shot.*

D. *Claircognizance* (knowing or understanding with clarity)

This is when you just know that something is true. Period. You receive information out of the blue from the spiritual world.

> *I was at home sitting on our sofa in the living room when my husband smiled and told me he had already bought me a present for my birthday, which was a month later. As soon as he said so, I <u>knew</u> that it had to do with pearls but I didn't say anything. A few days after, my daughter Valentina who loves keeping secrets (Marco had told her what he had bought for me), started teasing me, asking me to guess what the present was. I told her that it was round and white. She turned pale and didn't reply. My birthday came and when I opened my husband's gift I found a pair of beautiful pearl and gold pendant earrings!*

How did man evolve in the physical world?

After creating the fauna and the flora, we – the Creator's energetic extensions – co-created the human body in order to experience life and continue to co-create in the physical world. The human body didn't look like it appears to us today but evolved through the human conception of time.

What is the aura?

The physical body is surrounded and interpenetrated by the aura, a field of light that is the external manifestation of our soul's energy. It is an electromagnetic field of energy that extends from an average of about 3 feet (1 m) to a maximum of about 7 feet (2.1 m) from the physical body on all sides, depending on the person's physical, emotional and spiritual state.

The aura is made up of seven different interpenetrating layers or energy bodies, each of which vibrates at different frequencies. The reason we have more than one body is so that our spirit can interact in the different vibrational planes of the Universe, though most people are only aware of and use their physical body.

The physical body is the densest, which means that it vibrates at the lowest frequency compared to our other bodies. It is the vehicle used to explore the physical world.

Each of the seven subtle energy bodies are connected to a specific chakra (energy center). These energy centers basically convey energy from the non-physical to the physical dimension.

The seven layers or energy bodies that make up the aura are called in many different ways depending on the various cultures and beliefs.

•*First energy body (Etheric Body)*

This body is the first non-physical body and vibrates at a higher frequency than the physical body. It extends from one quarter of an inch (half cm) to 2 inches (5 cm) beyond the physical body. It is the exact duplicate of the physical body and it's associated to the 5 physical senses, including physical pleasure and pain. The Etheric Body is connected to the 1st energy center (chakra), called Muladhara or the Root Chakra.

Second energy body (Emotional Body)

This body vibrates at a higher frequency and is more thought-responsive than the Etheric Body. It extends from 1 inch (2.5 cm) to 3 inches (7.5 cm) from the physical body. Associated with emotions and feelings – such as fear, anger and love - the Emotional Body is connected to the 2nd energy center (chakra), called Svadhistana or the Sacral Chakra.

Third energy body (Mental Body, Lower Mental, Intellectual or Thought Energy Body)

This body vibrates at a higher frequency and is more thought-responsive than the Emotional Body. It extends from 3 inches (7.5 cm) to 8 inches (20 cm) from the physical body. Associated with thoughts and rational mental processes, it is connected to the 3rd energy center (chakra), called Manipura or the Solar Plexus Chakra.

Fourth energy body (Astral Body)

This body vibrates at a higher frequency and is more thought-responsive than the Mental Body. It extends from 6 inches (15 cm) to 12 inches (30 cm) from the physical body. Associated with love and relationships, it is connected to the 4th energy center (chakra), called Anahata or the Heart Chakra. This is the body that we use at night during sleep and that some consciously use for astral travel. This is also the same body that we use when our physical body dies.

Fifth Energy body (Etheric Template Body)

This body vibrates at a higher frequency and is more thought-responsive than the Astral Body. It extends from one and a half feet (45 cm) to 2 feet (60 cm) from the physical body. Associated with the Divine will, it is connected to the 5th energy center (chakra), called Vishuddha or the Throat Chakra.

Sixth energy body (Celestial, Cosmic or Heavenly Body)
This body vibrates at a higher frequency and is more thought-responsive than the Etheric Template Body. It extends from 2 feet (60 cm) to 2 and a half feet (75 cm) from the physical body. It is associated with divine, unconditional love and spiritual ecstasy. The Celestial Body is connected to the 6th energy center (chakra), called Anja or the Third Eye Chakra.

Seventh energy body (Causal Body, Ketheric Template)
This body vibrates at a higher frequency and is more thought-responsive than the Celestial Body. It is associated with the Divine mind and the full realization that We Are One. It extends from 2 and a half feet (75 cm) to 3 and a half feet (105 cm) from the physical body. The Causal Body is connected to the 7th energy center (chakra), called Sahasrara, the Crown Chakra.

What are chakras?
Chakras are energy centers. They are portals between the spiritual and the physical worlds. Our body has seven main chakras that are located along our spinal cord and at the top of our head. Universal life force enters our body through the chakras, which regulate the flow of energy in our system. If we are in good

physical and mental health, our chakras spin, allowing universal energy to enter. Blockage (caused by our negative emotions, such as anxiety, fear, sadness...) or imbalance of the chakras disrupts the flow of universal energy in our body, resulting in physical and mental ailments if left unaddressed. Each chakra is associated to determinate parts of the body and to determinate emotions. Each chakra is also associated with a determinate color as the chakras vibrate at different frequencies.

• **1st chakra: Muladhara, the Root Chakra** – located at the base of the spinal cord
Color: red energy
Parts of the body it influences: spine, hips, legs, feet, large intestine, sexual organs, adrenal glands, central nervous system, urinary system, skin, blood
Emotions it influences: basic survival needs, safety
Balanced 1st chakra: good health in the parts of the body it influences, prosperity and the feeling of safety
Blocked 1st chakra (emotional problems): anxiety, loss of self confidence, frustration, fear, insecurity, indecision, anger, resentment
Blocked 1st chakra (physical problems): bad health in the parts of the body it influences, including weight problems, sexual problems, intestinal ailments, knee problems, sciatica...

• **2nd chakra: Svadhistana, the Sacral Chakra** – located about 2 inches/5 cm under the navel
Color: orange energy
Parts of the body it influences: lower back, reproductive organs, kidneys, bowels, immune system

Emotions it influences: self-esteem, friendliness, creativity

Balanced 2nd chakra: good health in the parts of the body it influences, satisfied sexually

Blocked 2nd chakra (emotional problems): sexual problems, difficulty in relaxing

Blocked 2nd chakra (physical problems): bad health in the parts of the body it influences, including kidney problems, constipation, stiff lower back, bladder problems, muscle spasms...

• **3rd chakra: Manipura, the Solar Plexus Chakra** – located about 2 inches/5 cm above the navel

Color: yellow energy

Parts of the body it influences: digestive system, liver, spleen, gall-bladder, stomach, pancreas, small intestine

Emotions it influences: will power, self-esteem, self-control

Balanced 3rd chakra: good health in the parts of the body it influences, gratitude, energy, efficiency

Blocked 3rd chakra (emotional problems): anger, anxiety, depression, addiction, loneliness, eating disorders

Blocked 3rd chakra (physical problems): bad health in the parts of the body it influences, including digestive problems, liver problems, diabetes, food allergies, extra weight in the middle, ulcers, nervous breakdown

• **4th chakra: Anahata, the Heart Chakra** – located at the center of the chest

Color: green energy

Parts of the body it influences: chest, heart, upper back, arms, hands

<u>Emotions it influences</u>: love, empathy, compassion, spirituality, kindness

<u>Balanced 4th chakra</u>: good health in the parts of the body it influences

<u>Blocked 4th chakra (emotional problems)</u>: lack of compassion, indecisive, fear of being hurt, paranoid, jealousy, envy, hate, inability to forgive, lack of confidence

<u>Blocked 4th chakra (physical problems)</u>: bad health in the parts of the body it influences, including heart problems, breathing problems, immune system disorders, lung disease, circulation problems

- **5th chakra: Vishuddha, the Throat Chakra** – located at the base of the neck

<u>Color</u>: light blue energy

<u>Parts of the body it influences</u>: throat, ears, jaw, neck, shoulders, metabolism, teeth, thyroid and parathyroid glands

<u>Emotions it influences</u>: communication, sincerity, self-expression, creativity

<u>Balanced 5th chakra</u>: good health in the parts of the body it influences, skill of speaking and writing well, musical or artistic inspiration

<u>Blocked 5th chakra (emotional problems)</u>: shy, reserved, incapable of expressing feelings and thoughts, tendency of lying, fear of not being understood

<u>Blocked 5th chakra (physical problems)</u>: bad health in the parts of the body it influences, including hyperthyroidism, ear infections, throat ailments, breathing problems

• **6th chakra: Anja, the Third Eye Chakra** – located between the two eyebrows
<u>Color</u>: indigo energy
<u>Parts of the body it influences</u>: eyes, nose, central nervous system, cerebellum, face, lymphatic system, endocrine system
<u>Emotions it influences</u>: psychic vision, intuition
<u>Balanced 6th chakra</u>: good health in the parts of the body it influences, telepathy, astral travel, not attached to material things
<u>Blocked 6th chakra (emotional problems)</u>: can't remember dreams, refusal of all that is spiritual, mental confusion, sleeping disorders, loss of memory
<u>Blocked 6th chakra (physical problems)</u>: bad health in the parts of the body it influences, including headache, eye problems, epilepsy, sinusitis

• **7th chakra: Sahasrara, the Crown Chakra** – located at the top of the head
<u>Color</u>: purple energy
<u>Parts of the body it influences</u>: upper part of the head, brain, nervous system
<u>Emotions it influences</u>: cosmic awareness, spirituality
<u>Balanced 7th chakra</u>: good health in the parts of the body it influences, spiritual connection, knowledge, wisdom, mysticism
<u>Blocked 7th chakra (emotional problems)</u>: loneliness, depression, fear, frustration, unhappiness, thoughts of suicide
<u>Blocked 7th chakra (physical problems)</u>: bad health in the parts of the body it influences, including headache

What do the colors that you see in your mind's eye mean?

When you are meditating or when Reiki or other holistic practices are being done to you, you might see colors in your mind's eye. The colors that you see are energy colors. These are beautiful, intense colors that have DEPTH. They cannot be compared to the colors that we normally see. You see the color because the corresponding chakra is opening.

In June 2016 I attended a summer solstice event at Borgo Shanti, a holistic center near my house. At a certain point during the ceremony, the participants stood in a circle on the grass and chanted the Om sound. I did so too and closed my eyes. To my amazement I saw a beautiful red color in my mind, then I saw an intense orange. I opened my eyes to see if rays of sunlight were pointing at my eyes, therefore altering colors for me, but they weren't. Was it me or was it the Om sound, I wondered? I closed my eyes again - but this time in silence while the others continued to repeat Ommmm - and I again saw a gorgeous tone of red, then brilliant orange, then intense yellow, then a hint of green. I was pretty ignorant of chakras at the time but I later realized the Om sound and the energy of the group had opened my first three chakras and had begun to open the fourth.

*****

The first time I did Reiki to my mom, she saw the color purple when I had my hands over her head - that is, over her 7th chakra. Very often, the people to whom I give Reiki energy see colors in their mind's eye during the sessions.

> *During the last holistic fair I went to, I decided to try foot reflexology, which I had never done before. Throughout the 20 minutes of the treatment, I saw beautiful red, orange and yellow colors.*
> *****
> *Both my mom and I went to an osteopath who also uses the cranialsacral technique. We both saw purple in our mind's eye during the treatments. Seeing purple means connection to the spiritual world.*
> *****
> *Almost every time I do Hatha Yoga, I now see chakra colors: sometimes blue and purple, other times red and orange, and just once bright green.*
> *****
> *The only time I have ever seen the color gold was when I was doing Kriya yoga exercises.*

When holistic practitioners instead see colors while they are doing treatments, it could mean that energy is needed in the related chakra. Therefore, if a practitioner sees the color green, energy is required in the person's heart chakra.

Does the biblical silver cord exist?
The silver cord mentioned in the Bible is sometimes visible during out-of-body experiences. It connects the physical body to the 1st subtle energy body (also called Etheric Body). When this cord is broken, the physical body dies.

Can I see my aura?
The existence of the aura was proven scientifically by Walter John Kilner in 1911. In 1939 Semyon Kirlian

and his wife Valentina instead invented a system that they thought photographed the aura, but it actually captures the electromagnetic field around the body. There are also Aura Imaging Cameras that use biofeedback technology to offer an interpretation of what the aura could look like. These devices perceive the vibrations of the person and translate these into colors. The aura cannot be photographed as of yet (2019), but researchers, such as Daniele Gullà in Italy, are making progress in this field.

Some very sensitive people can see auras. By looking at someone's aura, they can tell if the person is kind or unkind, loving or hateful, generous or stingy...

Are there procedures to "clean" the aura?
You are the only one who can "clean" your aura. The best way to do this is to stay clear from entertaining negative thoughts and emotions, such as hate, envy, jealousy, greed, unkindness... Also stay clear from others having negative thoughts, words or deeds. Meditation, walks in the fresh air, bathing in salt water and a healthy diet are also helpful.

What do the colors emanating from the aura of a living person mean?
Auras are multicolored, but one color is usually dominant. It would take an entire book to describe all the nuances and their relative meanings but here are the basics:

Red (bright)	Full of energy, passionate, practical, hardworking, physical, enthusiastic, determined, sensual, moody, competitive, materialistic, powerful.

Red (deep)	Grounded to the earth, good adaptability, leadership, realistic, strong will power.
Red (muddy)	Anger, anxiety, egotism, sensuality, stinginess.
Pink (bright)	Loving, cheerful, friendly, sensitive, artistic, in love, intuitive, good balance between the material world and spiritual awareness, naive, warm-hearted.
Pink (dark)	Immature, dishonest, untrustworthy, deceitful.
Orange (bright)	Good health, dynamic, generous, loyal, sociable, excitement, creative, brave, battling a bad habit.
Orange-red	Authoritarian, self-confident.
Orange-yellow	Perfectionist, logical, intelligent, generous but expecting something in return.
Orange-brown	Excessive pride, laziness.
Yellow (gold)	Spiritual awakening, inspired, joyful, freedom-loving, easy-going, intelligent, generous... A yellow halo around the head means high spiritual development, a spiritual teacher.
Yellow (bright/lemon)	Fear of loss (of health, a job, a relationship).
Yellow (pale)	Beginning to awaken spiritually, excitement, optimistic, indecisive.
Yellow (muddy)	Mentally stressed out, need for attention/recognition, materialistic, egotistic.
Green (emerald)	Sociable, balanced, serene, doctor, healer or in the phase of being healed, teacher, green thumb, love of nature, love of animals.

Green (yellowish)	Creative, communicative.
Green (muddy)	Unreliable, jealous, resentful, low self-esteem, hypocrite, blames others.
Blue (royal)	Balanced, calm, clairvoyant, generous, highly spiritual, honest, intuitive, helpful, loving, supportive.
Blue (light)	Truthful, peaceful, good communicator.
Blue (dark/navy)	Fear of the future, fear of facing or speaking the truth.
Turquoise	Powerful healer or counselor, sensitive, well-organized, capable of influencing others, compassionate.
Indigo	Intuitive, sensitive, deep inner feelings, inner knowing.
Purple	Spiritual thoughts, visionary, mystic, futuristic, charismatic, artistic, magical, spiritual love, idealistic.
Silver	Physical and spiritual wealth.
Gold	Protected and guided by angels or other divine entities, wisdom, spiritual mind, intuitive thinker.
Black	Negative feelings, unforgiving, health problems, anger, hate.
Gray	Dark thoughts, depressed, distrustful, exhausted, sad, fearful, blocked energy.
Brown	Grounded, love of nature, materialistic, repressed, insecurity.
White	Purity, high spirituality, angelic qualities.
Rainbow (rainbow-colored rays)	Highly spiritually evolved, healer.

Do animals have auras and souls?

All animals have auras, including the smallest insects.

All animals, not just pets, also have souls and are eternal beings. Like us humans, they possess consciousness and use biological vehicles (their animal bodies) to experience the physical world.

Animals however differ from us in some ways, for example they live more in the moment than we do and are therefore more aligned with non-physical energy than we are.

Do plants have auras and souls?

All plants do have auras.

They however do not have souls, but they do possess intelligence and consciousness.

Is water intelligent?

Everything in the Universe, including every drop of water, possesses intelligence and consciousness.

Dr. Masaru Emoto (1943-2014) was a Japanese scientist who studied how the molecular structure of water changes when it is exposed to human words, sounds and thoughts. His book "The Hidden Messages in Water" explains how beautiful crystals are formed after water is exposed to kind words, harmonic music or prayers, while aesthetically ugly crystals are formed in the presence of angry words or dissonant music. Since the percentage of water in our bodies vary from 55-80% depending on our age, imagine the impact of this discovery on us human beings. Dr. Emoto's studies demonstrate how external influences - including the thoughts and words of others - have very radical repercussions on the human body and also in the environment in which we live.

Are the cells of my body intelligent?
Definitely so. Our body is made up of intelligent cells living in harmony with each other. It is only when we are not aligned with Who We Really Are that we interfere with our body's cellular balance, which leads to illness.

What is the structure of the Universe?
The Universe is multidimensional and interconnected. There are different planes of existence existing simultaneously that are however invisible to one another because each plane of existence has a distinct density or vibrational frequency.

The physical world is the densest, lowest-vibrating plane and the slowest thought-responsive plane, which means that it takes more time and more intense emotion to manifest in the physical than in the other dimensions. The physical world is therefore the perfect training ground for souls.

For more information on the different planes of existence, see page 156: "Which are the planes of existence?".

How does man contribute to the expansion of the Universe?
Man's thoughts and desires contribute to the expansion of the Universe. There has to be a reason for the expansion of the Universe and of eternity (the extended present) - and man's thoughts and desires are one of those reasons. The contrasts we experience in the physical world prompt us to have new desires which are perceived by our Creator and answered by Him, and if we are focused and aligned with our

desire, we manifest our desires in the physical world. This causes the Universe to expand.

We are indeed precious and brave citizens of the Universe! Without the contrasts we experience and our subsequent desires and manifestations, the Universe would no longer expand and would cease to exist.

What is time?

The past and the future do not exist outside of the physical world. Only the extended present exists in the other planes of the Universe. A hologram best describes this state of events: the past, present and future exist simultaneously. The subdivision of time into the past, present and future is only used by man in the physical world to measure the deterioration of physical matter.

In the spiritual planes of existence, immortal souls are free to go at any time to any point of time without any lapse in time – whether past or future in human terms.

What is space?

Space is not emptiness. Emptiness doesn't exist in the Universe. What we perceive as empty space is actually yet another of the Creator's co-creations. Our limited physical senses do not however allow us to understand, observe and appreciate everything that exists in the Universe.

Is there life on other planets in the Milky Way galaxy?

Planet Earth is just one of the numerous places where spirits can express themselves in a physical body.

What led to the creation of the physical universe?

Our Creator was not the sole creator of the Universe but it was us, His energetic extensions, who co-created the physical universe. Through thought and intense emotion, we jointly created physical matter. At first, we beheld the light that we were and created light in the physical form, the suns. Through the eons, we created the planets, water, living organisms, plants, animals, man... Every atom of substance, every cell in our body is the result of a combination of thought, emotion and desire.

How is the non-physical plane of existence different from the physical plane?

The physical world is the densest plane of existence, which means that it vibrates at the lowest frequency. It is the slowest thought-responsive plane, so it takes more time for thoughts to translate into manifestations. The non-physical plane instead progressively vibrates at a higher frequency and is increasingly thought-responsive as we come closer to the Creator - pure energy, pure thought, pure love.

How do spirits view life on Earth?

The physical world is the perfect environment in which to experience contrast and co-create, as it is the slowest thought-responsive plane, so it takes a lot of focused thought combined with emotion to be able to manifest. Many souls however consider living on Earth too harsh, since it is a world of conflict and too much diversity among the many inhabitants. These therefore choose other planes of existence in which to evolve. Those who instead choose the physical world are considered brave co-creators.

What are the laws that rule our Universe?

A. Our current *collective* reality is the result of what we have co-created in other planes of existence and in our previous and current physical lifetimes

It was the spiritual part of us – the Creator's energetic extensions - who co-created the physical world through focused thought and emotion. Through the ages of time, we co-created the sun (actually more than one), the planets, water, living organisms, plants, animals, the human body and everything else existing on this physical plane of existence.

B. *Part* of your current *personal* reality is what you – and no one else – established before coming into this physical plane of existence (your Life Project)

Before coming into the physical world, each of us pre-established certain life lessons or events in our lifetime as an opportunity to experience, learn from and spiritually evolve from these. So these pre-established events - which may be based on lessons that we failed to learn in previous lives or new challenges we wanted to experience - take place at some point of our lifetime. It could be, for example, that we choose a physical body that is genetically disadvantaged, or that we are born in a country riddled with war, or that we are instead born into a very rich family... The contrasts and situations we experience provoke desires, which we are able to turn into manifestations by matching the vibrational frequency of what we desire, as well as through focused thought combined with emotion. Whether you learn from the life lessons that you pre-established before coming to the physical world depends entirely on you.

C. *Part* of your current *personal* reality is what you have attracted into your current life (*The Law of Vibrational Attraction* and the *Law of Focused Thought Manifestation*)

Everything in the Universe produces an energetic vibration and our words, actions, and even our emotions and thoughts (the *cause*) have a consequence (the *effect*), whether it is intentional or unintentional. The *Law of Vibrational Attraction* says that vibrations of the same frequency attract each other (like attracts like), which means that if you are kind you will attract a person, situation or event into your personal reality that is a vibrational match to kindness. If you feel poor, you cannot attract richness. If you constantly talk about violence, you will experience and see it everywhere. It is you who attract your rewards and your punishments through your words, actions, thoughts and feelings, somewhat like a magnet attracts iron. Once you realize that you attract the corresponding effect of your words, actions, thoughts and feelings, you can stop attracting negative people and events and instead start consciously/intentionally attracting positive people and events into your personal reality. Through your positive words, thoughts and actions, you will attract the vibrational match of what you are emanating.

Owing to the *Law of Focused Thought Manifestation,* you also attract circumstances and events into your personal life experience when your thoughts are concentrated on someone or something, whether it is something that you consider desirable or undesirable.

By focusing your attention - your thoughts - on something, you end up attracting it (or something very similar) into your personal life experience.

D. The Law of Free Will

Our Creator gave us the gift of free will so that we could be free to be, do or have anything we pleased. We are powerful co-creators who through our focused thoughts and consequent manifestations in the physical world contribute to the continuous expansion of the Universe.

Each soul is entirely responsible for itself. You are the creator of your personal reality. You alone write your past, present and future.

In September 2016, my daughter convinced me to go all the way to Switzerland to have a past-life regression experience with Gustav Birth. The light hypnosis session lasted over 3 hours and I caught interesting glimpses of my previous lives. What however was especially enlightening was when I was brought to the presence of the Council of Elders after dying the last time (therefore in my life between lives). They were about 6 or 7 in all and had light coming from above their heads. I saw myself kneeling in front of them. The first Elder was dressed like a Franciscan friar, with a brown robe and a rope belt. He took my hands and helped me stand up. The friar then whispered into my ear: "Do not listen to others. Listen only to yourself." Then he gave me a roll of papyrus. I unrolled it and noticed that the texture of the paper was rough and had black archaic writing on it that I couldn't decipher. I knew that it represented my past. I

> *thanked the friar, who stepped aside and gave way to another Elder, who gave me another roll of paper. I unrolled it and saw that this was a smooth brand-new sheet of paper from which emanated a divine light. This papyrus represented the future - my future which was only up to me to decide and write.*

E. The Law of One

Every citizen of the Universe and everything existing in the physical world as well as in the other planes of existence is made of intelligent energy. The Creator is in everyone and everything.

F. The Law of Love

Love is the beginning and the end. It is our soul's highest aspiration. Every time we do not see someone through the eyes of Love, for any reason, we enter into conflict with the Universe and with Who We Really Are.

G. The Law of Everlasting Life

Everything in the physical world (and indeed in the Universe) - including humans, fauna, flora and physical objects - is made up of energy that never dies, but simply changes form. Our spirits are eternal. When our physical body dies, our spirits re-emerge in the non-physical dimension. Death does not exist – we never cease to be.

Are the universal laws valid even for those who do not believe in them?
Absolutely so.

What is reality in the physical world?

We have two co-existing realities in the physical world: our current *collective* reality (objective reality) and our current *personal* reality (subjective reality).

• Current *collective* reality:

This is the result of what we – our Creator's energetic extensions - have co-created up to now in other planes of existence and in previous and current physical lifetimes. Everything existing in the physical plane of existence, including the planets, gravity, plants, animals, the human body and all matter, have been co-created by us through focused thought and emotion.

• Current *personal* reality:

Part of your current personal reality is what you - and you alone - established before coming into this physical plane of existence (your Life Project). Before coming into the physical world, each of us decided we would experience certain circumstances or events in our lifetime in order to learn from these experiences and evolve spiritually.

Another part of your current personal reality is what you have consciously or unconsciously, intentionally or unintentionally, attracted in your current life through the *Law of Vibrational Attraction* and the *Law of Focused Thought Manifestation*.

Everything in the Universe produces an energetic vibration, including your words, actions, and even your feelings and thoughts. So each individual vibrates at a different frequency, depending on what he/she thinks, feels, says and does. By the *Law of Vibrational Attraction*, vibrations of the same frequency attract each other (like attracts like), so you attract positive events if you think, feel, say and do positive things and you attract negative events if you think, feel, say and do negative things.

With the *Law of Focused Thought Manifestation*, you instead attract what you focus your attention on, so your focused thoughts and intentions, combined with emotion, *also* create and shape your personal reality. Therefore, if you focus your attention on something unwanted, you will end up attracting that same unwanted situation (or something very similar).

How do thoughts affect reality?
Matter and events do not happen of their own accord. Nothing in our lives appears or happens unless we have invited it into our reality. It is in fact we who create our personal reality through the vibrations we emit (like attracts like) through focused thought. And every person as well as every person's thought or idea vibrates at a particular frequency. When we first have an idea or thought, the vibration isn't usually very high, but if we continue to have this idea or thought and experience profound emotion, the vibration becomes more intense and we begin to attract - like a magnet - something regarding this idea into our life experience. We could for example "happen to" meet people that are connected some way with our thought or idea, or see something oddly pertinent to our idea in Internet, in a magazine, or elsewhere.

> *One day I was thinking of how nice it would be to have a big house where I could live with my husband and son and also with my Mom, my daughter and her family. The next day, my son chose for us to see together - of all the films in the world - "Gone with the Wind", where there is a beautiful, enormous plantation house called Tara.*

Before getting up from bed one morning I was imagining what it would feel like to win a million euros (never did this before). Then I got up, turned on my mobile phone and saw that I had received a spam (never received one before on my mobile) that said I had won a million British pounds.

Our continued focused, emotion-filled thoughts lead to our experiencing the corresponding physical manifestation.

I was looking through a fashion magazine and saw a lovely top that cost a fortune, entirely made with opalescent pink sequins. It's very rare that I see something not only that I like but that I think would look good on me... So I cut out the image - but thought "I will never pay that kind of money for a top" - and put it into a "magic" box where I keep ideas of what I would like to do or have one day. A few days later I took a walk downtown and saw what looked like the very same opalescent pink sequin top in a boutique. But a closer look revealed that it was even prettier than the one in the magazine, that it had a different label and that it cost lots less and it was even discounted by 30%, so it was actually incredibly cheap!
*****
One Sunday morning I was busy making pancakes and my mind was absorbed in thinking of making more and more pancakes... The next day I received a text message from the mom of one of my students saying that 11 year old Matteo had just discovered what pancakes were and that he wanted to make some with me during our next English lesson.

I was finishing lunch with my husband and he mentioned Gaeta. I went on and on about how beautiful Gaeta is, that I adore Gaeta and that one day I'm going to live there. A few minutes later, my brother phoned saying he wanted to invite my mom and me to go for a trip to Gaeta that summer!

*****

Upon my insistence, my son-in-law went to the Emergency Room (and he fortunately listened to me) and during the same week I accompanied my daughter and granddaughter twice to the Emergency Room for other health-related issues. The next day I was taking a walk on the main street and a young girl on a bicycle stopped and asked me - of all the people who were walking by at that time: "Where is the Emergency Room?"

We are powerful creators and have been given the gift of manifesting physical objects and events through focused thought. Unfortunately, if we focus our thoughts on things/events that we do not want, we can attract those even though we do not want them... We are 100% responsible for our thoughts, words and actions because our thoughts, words and actions create our personal reality.

What are thought forms?

Each and every thought we have vibrates at a specific frequency and radiates from us into the Universe. Even though we are currently in the physical world, where it us takes longer and/or more focused attention than in other planes of existence to mold energy and manifest desires, we do have that ability! If we maintain focus, our thought accumulates energy and can actually be seen by sensitives or astral travelers, appearing as vaporous clouds. At first these thought forms have hazy outlines but as the thought continues to be focused and intense, the thought forms become increasingly distinguishable and eventually this accumulated energy manifests itself in the physical world.

How do thought forms turn into physical events and physical matter?

Everything in the Universe produces an energetic vibration, including thoughts. Everything in the physical world originates from a simple thought. Once the thought - combined with emotion - emanates from us and accumulates energy, it is transformed into a thought form in the spiritual world. All matter is made of light. And all light comes from the Creator.

MY PERSONAL REALITY

What makes a happy person?

Happiness is a spiritual condition that is measured by the amount of joy that we experience during our life. It is a state of mind that is not influenced by external events. In fact, to be happy one does not necessarily have to be economically rich, have an influential job or lead a glamorous life, though it is true that those who are happy can easily attract those circumstances into their life experience if they desire so.

Once we satisfy our basic needs - air, water, food, shelter, clothing, education and good personal relationships - we do not need any other ingredient to be happy. By showing love, being kind to others, being joyful and grateful for what we have and by enjoying life as it is, with its beautiful moments and its contrasts that force us to grow and learn, we can reach that glorious spiritual condition.

Do I create my own personal reality?

We are the sole creators of our own personal realities. No one and nothing else is responsible for the events taking place in our lives, for the type of people we meet, for our body's health...

It is our own thoughts and emotions that mold our personal reality, that attract and manifest all the circumstances and events in our life experience. Everything in the Universe produces an energetic vibration and our words, our actions, our emotions and our thoughts (the *cause*) have a consequence (the *effect*). We have been given the gift of free will so that we could be free to be, do or have anything we pleased through focused thought combined with emotion. Each soul is entirely responsible for itself. We alone write our past, present and future.

So what are your current thoughts? How do you usually feel emotionally, what are the words you usually speak and the deeds you usually do? These are all creating your future! Your thoughts can lead you to future happiness or misery, success or failure, health or disease.

You are 100% responsible for your life and once you realize the power you have, you can intentionally create the future you desire by deliberately directing your thoughts on what you want: good health, love, peace of mind, good relationships, prosperity...

What tool can help me create the reality I desire?
Your mind is a treasure! It is the tool you use to create a happy or unhappy life. Each and every one of us has the power to create the life we choose simply by using the creative power of our minds. We are the powerful creators of our own existences.

If it's my mind that creates the reality I desire, of what use is my body?
The physical world is the perfect training ground for souls since this is the densest, lowest-vibrating plane and the slowest thought-responsive plane, which means that it takes more time and more emotion to manifest in the physical than in the other dimensions. We have been temporarily given a physical body so that we can have experiences in the physical world and enjoy and learn from these.

Should I go with the tide or steer my life?
We are blessed with the powerful gift of being able to create our personal reality through our thoughts and emotions, and it would be sad to waste this gift and passively go with the tide, being at the mercy of anyone or anything coming our way through our unconscious thoughts and emotions – or worse yet, if someone else steered our life based on their desires rather than our own. It would be as if we disowned the fact that we are divine sparks. Our life however is ours to do whatever we desire, as we have also been given the gift of free will.

How can I gain more control of my life experience?
Ask yourself at different moments of the day: "What do I want right now? What do I desire this very moment?" Take note of the thoughts and emotions you have during the day. If your thoughts and emotions are not positive ones, tell yourself: "In this moment I intend finding a thought that makes me feel better."

Someone wants to control my life, saying it's for my good. What should I do?
You are a spark of the Creator and a powerful co-creator just as everyone else on Earth. Though friends or family members are trying to be helpful, no one knows better than you what is good for you and what is bad for you – *unless you are not paying attention to your inborn emotional guidance system*. Only you and no one else has the power to manifest your desires. What good would it do to you to manifest someone else's desires? Turn your attention away from the person trying to control your life and follow the *Wish*

Come True Technique (see page 41) to manifest what *you* want.

Why do I need to pay extreme attention to my emotions?

Our emotions are indicators of where we are in relation to our spiritual essences and also reveal whether we are aligned or not with our desires. We can clearly see from the type of emotion we have if our thoughts, words and deeds are in harmony with our true nature and our true life intents. When we experience a negative emotion - such as discomfort, sadness, jealousy, fear, lack of... - that means that we are directing our attention to something that we don't want and that we are also attracting something that we don't want into our future. When we instead have a positive emotion - such as joy, optimism, gratitude, abundance... - that means that we are directing our attention to something that we do want plus we are attracting something that we desire into our personal life experience. If we pay attention to how we feel, we can consciously change the direction of our thoughts, turning our minds to more positive aspects (even if that involves ignoring current reality), so that we can feel better. In that case, our vibrations change and we can begin to attract what we desire.

Do I attract everything that is in my reality?

The circumstances and events in your life have been invited into your personal reality by you - and you alone - either through your thoughts, words or deeds (like attracts like) or through your focused attention to someone or something. However, part of your current personal reality is also what you - and you alone -

established before coming into this physical plane of existence (your Life Project). The people you meet, the events that you experience – indeed all of the positive and negative situations in your life - are the result of your thoughts, words and actions and/or your focused attention to someone or something and/or your Life Project. Absolutely nothing in our lives just "happens" – there is a reason for everything.

Examples of attraction through thoughts, words and deeds (Law of Vibrational Attraction): A person who is often irritable with others can attract a boss that humiliates him/her or another negative circumstance. A person who is generous can attract winning the lottery or another positive circumstance.

*****

Examples of attraction by focusing one's attention to someone or something (Law of Focused Thought Manifestation): a person close to a patient who consistently focuses his/her attention on this disease can attract the disease itself (or another disease) into his/her life experience. A child who observes his parents constantly fighting can attract ill health, a bully at school or another negative event.

*****

I was listening to an Abraham-Esther Hicks session on YouTube that was talking about how to lose weight and Twinkies were mentioned. This sweet snack isn't sold in Italy and it reminded me of my childhood, so I thought about Twinkies for a while, trying to remember how they were made and what they tasted like. Well, in less than an hour, I began watching a new TV series that mentioned Twinkies.

> *Someone I know very well broke the handle of his bedroom door when trying to close it upon leaving for Rome one morning. Later on in the day: he had a problem going out of the door of a movie theater in Rome; he had a problem going out of the door of Eataly; and he had a problem entering the door of the restaurant where he went for dinner.*
>
> *****
>
> *Example of Life Project:* A person chooses before coming into the physical plane of existence to understand what it feels like to be poor in order to learn from this experience. The person will continue to be poor until he/she has learned everything he/she needs to learn.

Your health issues, relationship problems and financial fiascos are the manifestation of your continued negative thoughts or you are dealing with an important life lesson that you pre-established before coming into the physical world. Whatever the cause, you can at any point change the situation by changing your thoughts, words and deeds.

Why do I experience negative events?
The reason you experience negative circumstances or events is that you have invited them into your life experience through:

- your continued negative thoughts, words or actions

- your focused attention to someone or something negative

- a lesson to learn in the Life Project you pre-established before being born

As we have the precious gift of free will, we are free at any time to change our personal reality, whatever is the cause of our negative experience.

Of what use are contrasts?

Contrasts encourage us to desire changes to our current life experience. We are constantly confronted with contrasts, which help us to pinpoint our personal preferences. In fact, in order to understand what we want, we have to experience what we don't want. In our strife to gain what we desire, we are contributing to the expansion of the Universe.

Do children, including babies, attract everything that is in their reality?

Children are no different from anyone else – they too are powerful creators of their personal life experience. They too have thoughts and emit vibrations based on these thoughts. They too invite positive and negative circumstances into their life experience through:

- their continued negative thoughts, words or actions (children are however much less likely to have continued negative thoughts, words or actions compared to adults);

- their focused attention to someone or something negative;

- a circumstance or event they pre-established in their Life Project before being born.

Do animals attract everything that is in their reality?

Animals are no different from humans in that they too create their personal life experience. Animals that are free and live in nature are more aligned with their spiritual essences - and therefore attract and manifest what they desire - than animals that are confined in zoos, farms or houses.

What practical steps can I take to fulfill my desire?
Follow the *__Wish Come True Technique__*:

1. Reflect on what is truly important for you.
What is it that you want and *need*? A true desire is a wish that your heart makes. Is your desire really yours or someone else's desire? Does thinking of fulfilling your desire make you feel happy?

2. Raise your vibrational frequency to the point of feeling joy and an open heart
Your emotions indicate whether you match the vibrational frequency of your desire or not. Be nice to others, joyful, grateful, caring, loving...

3. Ask the Universe for what you want in a very clear, detailed way
When you formulate your desire, your dream, describe what you want to the Universe in detail, and also specify why you want it.

Matthew, 7-8: "Ask and it will be given to you; seek and you will find; knock and the door will be opened to you. For everyone who asks receives; he who seeks finds; and to him who knocks, the door will be opened."

---

4. Visualize and feel the emotion of having what you asked for

By visualizing yourself getting what you asked for, as it were a movie, and actually feeling the emotion of having it, you are attracting it into your personal reality. Be creative – use your imagination! Dedicate 15 minutes of your time at night before sleep and/or before getting up in the morning to visualizing your dream come true. The more you focus your attention on your desire and feel the intense emotion of joy, gratitude, enthusiasm springing from your heart, the faster the manifestation will take place.

5. KNOW that what you have asked for will arrive and in your mind visualize yourself as having already received what you have asked for

Once you have asked for your desire, let it go... Do not keep on asking because you have already asked and the Universe has already heeded your request. Have faith that your desire will come to you, visualize in your mind as having already received what you have asked for and continue to be a vibrational match to your desire. As always, your emotions will tell you if you are aligned (in harmony) with your desire or not. If you are confident that it's on its way to you - you *expect* for it to arrive - and your thoughts, words and deeds are positive ones, you will soon manifest your desire in your personal reality. If you are instead doubtful or your thoughts, words and deeds are negative ones, you are preventing your desire from becoming a part of your life experience.

> *Mark, 11:24: "Therefore I tell you, whatever you ask for in prayer, believe that you have received it, and it will be yours."*

6. Live in the Here-and-Now

Life is not yesterday nor tomorrow, nor is it in some other place. Your life is right now and exactly where you are this very moment. It is now - and not later - that you can have thoughts, speak words and do actions that make you feel good, thus making you non-resistant to receiving what you desire. Living in the Here-and- Now while feeling good lets the flow of Universal Energy reach you. Thus relinquish your concerns about the future, turn off whatever negative thoughts you might have and completely immerse yourself in this moment in time and the place where you find yourself. It is only here and now that you can see the value of your present moment and place, whatever and wherever it may be.

7. Observe your thoughts when you are living in the Here-and-Now

You have already asked for your desire to come true so there is no need to repeat it as the Universe has already heard you. What you need to do now is to live in the Here-and-Now doing something else besides focusing on your desire, such as working, cooking, writing on your computer, gardening, whatever... and take note of:

- any thought that appears *unrelated* to what you are thinking about (for example, you are at the cash register and your mind is absorbed in counting out the money in front of the cashier...

and all of a sudden you think about a friend you haven't seen in a long time);

- where your eyes linger when you are doing something else (for example, you are in your car at a traffic light and you notice your eyes focusing a few seconds longer than usual on a sign);

- on which words your ears linger when you are doing something else (for example, you are at work and your mind is concentrated on your work ... and your attention is suddenly captured by the words said by someone at a nearby desk);

- your dreams.

Keep a diary of all these thoughts and dreams and you will gradually realize that you have the key to obtaining what you have been asking for. You will find that your "stray" thoughts, your dreams and the focused attention of your physical senses on apparently unrelated things give you an inspiration that helps you to achieve your desire. Some say that what's in play is intuition, an innate ability of ours to know something without using our five senses or our previous experiences, while others believe that it's instead our spirit guides, angels or others yet (inhabitants in the astral plane, both dead and alive) giving us help.

8. Take immediate action based upon the sign/intuition/inspiration you have received

Taking action is key. You are in the physical world and your next step is to do something - big or small - based on the sign/intuition/inspiration you have received. You are not meant to be a passive player but the protagonist of your life experience. If you don't take action, you are making it much more difficult for the Universe to materialize what you want. If, for example, you have asked the Universe for a new job working for a company, but you don't give your C.V. to anyone nor answer any job offers, you are obstructing the creative process. If you have dreamt of winning the lottery but don't get up from your couch to buy a lottery ticket, you are obstructing the creative process. Do not wait... act immediately upon receiving your sign/intuition/inspiration!

9. Thank the Universe

When you have received what you asked for – and you will if you have done the above – thank the Universe, be grateful for and enjoy what you have received.

What is intuition?

Intuitions are activated by our desires. An intuition is a thought that is unrelated to what we were thinking about when we had it. For example, we were thinking if we were giving the right amount of water to a plant when all of a sudden we think about something entirely different, such as a relative, a place, a number, a color... Intuitions are often - but not always - symbolic and not literal. The symbols used are very personal, so they do not apply to everyone, and they also need to be interpreted by you. The interpretation part can be quite tricky... as your logical mind can misinterpret what the intuition is telling you.

In May 2012, a series of very powerful earthquakes hit the town of Mirandola, located 20 miles away

> *from where I live. The effects of these quakes had repercussions also in my apartment building, with awful shaking and cracks on the floors and walls. So now, if I suddenly see in my mind's eye the image of Mirandola, this symbolizes "earthquake" for me. When Mirandola comes to my mind, it either means that an earthquake will happen fairly close to home or that something in my life will be greatly disrupted.*

Remember that there is a reason for every thought we have. There is a reason, a meaning, if our eyes or our ears or our nose has noticed something. I strongly advise you to create your own symbol dictionary!

> *I was in my car at a traffic light thinking: "How can I lose weight?" and "What diet should I try next?" I noticed my eyes lingering on the sign of a grocery shop, with the picture of a squirrel. I later Googled "squirrel diet" and discovered that they eat nuts, seeds, mushrooms, avocados, apples, apricots, corn, twigs and bark. Therefore the response was to eat fruits, vegetables and nuts.*
>
> *****
>
> *I have the habit of playing a euro or two on Lotto. One day I asked: "Did I win the Lotto?" The reply that I heard in my mind was: "Little Bo Beep has LOST her sheep". And lose I did.*
>
> *****
>
> *Another time I asked: "Will I win the Lotto tonight?" Then I saw the image of Charlie Pace, who was a fictional character in the TV series "Lost". And lose I did.*

Yet another time I asked: "Did I win the Lotto last night?" Then I suddenly thought back when I was 10 or 11 years old. I was in a museum, I think the Smithsonian, in Washington D.C. and I lost my silver bracelet while walking around. I went to the Lost & Found desk and someone had found the my bracelet! So I put it back on but a little bit later I realized that I had lost it again! I was too embarrassed to tell anyone that I had lost it again... So the message to me was: Yes, you've lost the Lotto again! And so I did.

*****

But I sometimes win using intuition... One time, for example, I saw actor Ewan McGregor in my mind so I played 71 (he was born in 1971), then I immediately thought of 46 (for no reason) and I won – not much, but I won!

What is the difference between a mind thought and an intuition?

It's easy to distinguish a mind thought from an intuition. Mind thoughts are connected to each other logically. You think of one thing that leads to another related thought that leads to another related thought. An intuition instead comes out of the blue and is unrelated to what you were thinking about.

What are examples of negative emotions that prevent you from achieving your desire?

Frustrated, jealous, anxious, fearful, hateful, angry, revengeful, unhappy, envious, nostalgic, depressed, critical, prejudiced, complaining, worried, blaming, sad, discouraged, greedy, bored, lack of self-confidence, guilt, despair, feeling of being helpless, feeling poor, unsatisfied, pessimistic, irritated, resentful, sense of insecurity, unworthiness, impatient, violent, paranoid, distrusting, uncertain, uncomfortable, disappointed, disorganized, stressed out, powerless, disrespectful...

What are examples of positive emotions that raise your vibrational frequency so that you can manifest what you desire?
Love, enthusiasm, pride, passion, certainty, powerful, happiness, optimism, hope, gratitude, appreciation, joy, satisfaction, peaceful, generousness, patience, feeling full of energy, comfortable, trustfulness, kindness, cheerfulness, excitement, self-confidence, awe, amusement, feeing rich, worthiness, organized, serene, respectful...

Can I formulate any desire?
As long as you ask for something that you truly want and *need,* you can formulate almost any desire, because anything the mind can imagine or conceive of has the possibility of existing, since our desires are received by the Universe and instantly answered. The desires that we cannot formulate are:

- desires that are in conflict with the laws of our current collective reality, such as gravity, the Earth spinning around the Sun... (thus we cannot fly with our physical body nor ask for the Sun to be hotter in winter);

- desires that involve limiting the freedom of other living beings (such as making an ex-spouse fall in love with you again or becoming better/more successful/richer than another person).

If I get what I desire, am I preventing someone else from getting what he/she wants?

We live in a Universe where there is unending abundance so there is no way that you can deprive someone else from getting what he/she wants. Everyone is responsible for their own personal life reality and has the means of manifesting their desires. All of our true wishes are heeded and granted by the Universe.

Is it more difficult to manifest a big desire compared with a little desire?

The same creative process is used to manifest big desires and little desires. We are usually less resistant though to little desires, so it's easier for us to attract a little money compared with a lot of money.

Isn't it silly to ignore my current reality and to use my imagination to manifest my desire?

You attract what you focus your attention on (combined with emotion), whether you are focusing on something that is real or on something that you have imagined. So no, it is not silly to ignore your current reality as by doing this, you can create your future the way you want it to be.

How long should I focus on my desire to be able to manifest it?

When we focus our attention on an idea or thought, there is a corresponding vibration that at first isn't usually very high. If we however continue (without interruption) to have this idea or thought and experience deep emotion for at least one minute, the idea or thought becomes dominant and the corresponding vibration becomes more intense and we begin to attract - like a magnet - something regarding this idea into our life experience. To be able to actually manifest the desire, we however need to follow the first 8 steps of the *Wish Come True Technique.* If we do so, we can obtain the manifestation of our desire even within a few minutes.

What changes do I experience when I start manifesting my desires?

When you begin to realize that you are divine sparks and understand the process of manifesting your desires, your life will inevitably change for the better. Your creative power will grow considerably. You will pay more and more attention to your emotions, becoming gradually more expert in blocking unwanted, negative thoughts and more expert in entertaining desirable, positive thoughts. You will find yourself formulating more and more desires – desires that you never thought or dared of having. As you experience these changes, you will inevitably attract people similar to what you have become and - for one reason or another - some people in your life may vanish from your scenario because you are no longer vibrationally in sync with them.

How can I tell if I am aligned with my desire?

Your emotions are perfect indicators of where you are in relation to what you have asked for. When you are thinking of your desire and you feel *any* negative emotion - such as impatience, doubt or fear - that means that you are not aligned with your desire and that you are preventing your desire from being manifested in your life experience. If on the other hand you think of your desire with joyful anticipation and you are feeling positive emotions, you are sure to attract it into your life.

How can I know when my vibrational frequency is low?

As always, let your emotions be the indicators of your vibrational frequency. Every time you experience a negative emotion, you can stop it from persisting in your here-and-now and instead consciously direct your attention to something that makes you feel good. A low vibrational frequency means that you're not aligned with your desire, so you are preventing yourself from getting what the Universe has already granted to you. By consciously improving the way you feel in your here-and-now, you can instead open the door and let the Universe's gift get into your life experience.

How can I raise my vibrational frequency?

E*verything* in the Universe produces an energetic vibration and our words, actions and thoughts (the *cause*) have a consequence (the *effect*). Once you realize that you attract the corresponding effect of your words, actions, thoughts and feelings, you can stop attracting negative people and events and instead start consciously/intentionally attracting positive people and events into your personal reality. The best way would be to completely eliminate negative emotions, but the contrasts we face do not always leave us joyful and enthusiastic. When we experience a contrast of any kind, what we can do is to find a thought that makes us feel better, so that we do not persist in feeling bad - which not only makes us feel awful but also prevents our desires to manifest. You can consciously choose a better thought that leads to another better thought... to the point that you raise your vibrational frequency to feeling good again.

At times though some contrasts are so hard to handle that it's best to turn your thoughts entirely away from the negative experience you are having - therefore to ignore your reality - and focus your mind on something else. Just step away...

You can avoid doing anything that makes you feel uncomfortable. You can choose to hang out with positive, loving people. You can choose to do things you enjoy doing. You can choose to be a better person.

TECHNIQUE TO RAISE YOUR VIBRATIONAL FREQUENCY

Buy a little notebook dedicated to this alone, get into a relaxed state of mind & body, then make a list of 40 things that open your heart. This may take days or even weeks to complete. Though what opens your heart is very individual, here are some examples to give you an idea:

∞ *Things that glitter and sparkle*
∞ *Holograms*
∞ *An ice cream at Slurp*
∞ *The full rainbow I saw on the Swiss lake*
∞ *Kaleidoscopes*
∞ *The song "I'm so pretty"*
∞ *Petting my cat Atena.*
∞ *The marvel felt upon seeing a spiritual being*
∞ *The scent of vanilla*

∞ *When my children call me "Mamma"*
∞ *Imagining myself lying on a sunbed on the beach*
∞ *The combination of pink and orange.*
∞ *The blossoming of the Japanese crabapple trees in front of the Esselunga supermarket.*
∞ *Singing.*
∞ *Stepping on the scale and discovering that I have lost some weight.*
∞ *The enormous red sun that was setting on the sea of Peschici.*
∞ *The beautiful sensation I felt when I meditated for the very first time: being One with the Universe*
Once you have completed your list, make sure you read it often – especially when you feel you need to boost your energy and raise your vibrations.

Why is it best to focus on my desire before falling asleep and upon awaking?

Right before falling asleep and immediately upon awaking, we are in a transitional state of consciousness, in between the physical and the astral worlds. In those transitional periods, called half-sleep, our subconscious minds are highly suggestible. One of the chief impediments to co-creating our reality is *not believing* that our dream can come true. As exposed in point 5 of the *Wish Come True Technique*, we cannot attract a circumstance or an event that we do not believe is possible. If we are doubtful - if we say "I want X, *but...*" - we are preventing our desire from becoming a part of our life experience. By focusing on our desire before sleep and upon awaking, we are basically making it easier for ourselves to realize that what we have asked for is possible to obtain. So remember to dedicate 15 minutes of your time at night before sleep and/or before getting up in the morning to thinking about your desire and visualizing your dream come true.

I am good at focusing on my desire but don't feel the joy that is required to getting what I want. What should I do?

The trick is to do something that makes you feel really good. The way to achieve the state of joy and an open heart is very individual. Taking a walk in nature, listening to music, painting, gardening... are just a few of the many options. The state of joy is a requirement for obtaining what you want – there is no way you can bypass it!

If I focus on something I don't want, do I attract it into my reality?

By focusing your thought on unwanted things, you unwittingly attract these unwanted things into your personal life experience. At first, you begin attracting relevant phenomena, such as a tv program talking about the unwanted circumstance or event, or you "happen" to meet someone somehow connected to the unwanted thing. Our continued focused, emotion-filled thoughts however lead us to eventually experiencing the corresponding physical manifestation even if it is unwanted.

Personal examples of attracting something unwanted:
One afternoon while I was going to pick up my son at school, I drove past a café where I saw a drug pusher standing in the nearby parking lot. I had been noticing drug dealers in the very same spot for ages selling hard drugs, and every time I passed by

there I wondered why no one had reported that. Was I the only one to notice things going on? As usual, I started imagining myself calling the police and thinking whether it was better to call the regular Police, the Municipal Police or the Carabinieri (military police). A few minutes later I was at a standstill at a red traffic light, then the light turned green and I was about to start going when the woman in the BMW behind me rammed into my car. My car at first glance didn't seem damaged much but then I started noticing that my neck hurt. Even though it was obviously the woman's fault, she was not sympathetic at all and just wanted to exchange phone numbers and go away, without filling out an accident statement for insurance purposes, as is usually done in Italy. My instincts told me that I needed to call someone for some help. By mistake, I called the Police, but the Carabinieri instead picked up the call (I know it seems odd but it's true) and then passed me over to the Municipal Police, who quickly came and helped me out. Fortunately so, because the mechanic and the insurance company established the damage at over 1,000 euros!

The point though is that I attracted this event. I attracted the fact that I had to get in touch in some way with all three types of law enforcement agencies.

*****

My daughter came to my house one afternoon and noticed that she had lost the back of her earring, the little part that secures the earring to the ear lobe. It was made of gold and we looked around for it for a few minutes but couldn't find it. The next

> *day I decided to have a good look in the living room and first swept the floor with a broom, then used a dust catcher with zero results. I eventually got down on my hands and knees, searching in every corner but couldn't find it. I wondered frustrated where it had disappeared to. The doorbell then rang and my student came in for an English lesson. Half way during the lesson, one of my earrings suddenly dropped on the table in front of us. I had lost the back part of my earring owing to the Law of Focused Thought Manifestation and I haven't found it yet...*

How can I eliminate something from my life experience that I don't want?

The only way to eliminate something from your personal reality that you don't want is to turn your attention away from the unwanted person, circumstance or event. You have the power to deliberately direct your thoughts to the people, circumstances and events that you do want.

How can I get rid of doubt that we are gods with the powerful gift of co-creating reality?

No one else can convince you that it is true that we have the power to co-create our personal life experiences. The best way for you to realize that it is true is to try the *Wish Come True Technique*. Start with something little, something that you believe is possible to achieve and then see what happens... Experiment the art of intentionally co-creating your future and a whole new world will open up for you.

What can help me to co-create my new reality if I am having a hard time using my imagination?

By visualizing yourself getting what asked for, as it were a movie, and actually feeling the emotion of having it, you are attracting it into your personal reality. Sit or lie in a quiet place, close your eyes and calm your mind (for example, meditate or count mentally) and imagine yourself getting what you desire.

If your desire involves getting a new car, close your eyes and imagine yourself walking into a car salon. A salesman comes up to ask what you're looking for but you say, "Do you mind if I take a look around?" He nods and walks back into his office, while you start looking at the beautiful shiny new cars lined up...

If you're however suffering from a lack of imagination, then try using someone else's imagination! You can for example read an excerpt from a book or watch a movie scene in which the protagonists achieve the same circumstance or event as you desire, such as finding love, getting a new car/house/job... *Feel the emotion* that the protagonists feel when they fall in love, when they enter the new house they bought, when they give birth to their long-wanted child, when they pass a very difficult test, when they climb the mountain that they deeply desired to climb...

I have tried the *Wish Come True Technique* for a fairly long time but my desire has not yet become a part of my reality. Why is that and what should I do?

- *Are you a vibrational match to what you desire?*

Vibrations of the same frequency attract each other (like attracts like), which means that if you are kind you will attract a person, situation or event into your personal reality that is a vibrational match to kindness. Make sure that your words, actions, thoughts and feelings are good, positive ones, which not only makes you a better person but also allows you to attract positive people and events into your personal reality as well as the object of your desire.

- *Do you truly believe that it is possible for you to get what you desire now or in the near future?*

If you are doubtful, you are preventing your desire from becoming a part of your life experience.

- *Have you taken action?*

If you haven't, you are making it far much more difficult for the Universe to materialize what you want. If, for example, you want to find a job but you don't give your C.V. to anyone, you don't tell anyone that you are looking for a job and you don't answer any job offers, you are obstructing the creative process. If you are dreaming of finding true love but you don't get out of the house and disconnect your communication devices, you are obstructing the creative process.

What I am experiencing in my current reality is blocking me from co-creating the reality I desire. What should I do?

Your current reality is the result of what you have previously co-created. But the good news is that you have the power to change the situation. If the circumstance in which you find yourself is really bad, it is advisable to turn your thoughts entirely away from the negative experience you are having - therefore to *ignore* your reality - and focus your mind on something else - anything else that makes you feel a little bit better, such as:

- watch a funny movie;

- get together with a dear friend (do *not* talk about your negative situation but if you do so, mention it very briefly and then change the subject);

- go for a walk and set your mind to noticing nice things – the warmth of the Sun, the smiling person you pass by, a child skipping happily, a flower, a leaf, a snowflake, a gorgeous outfit in a shop window, a beautiful decoration in front of someone's house, a dog wagging its tail...

By ignoring your reality – that is, distracting yourself from your reality – you are deliberately changing your Here-and-Now. If you continue to ignore your reality, you will find that you will be able to feel better and better, which will consequently allow you to attract positive circumstances and events into your life.

Can other people prevent me from co-creating my reality?

No one besides yourself can co-create your reality as it's your thoughts and feelings, your actions and your words that co-create your future. If you however allow yourself be influenced by someone else's thoughts or opinions or beliefs, you are handing over your creative power to that someone else and giving that other person the protagonist role of your life script...

The bad news I hear about is preventing me from having positive thoughts. What should I do?

Internet is extraordinary, as we can now instantly access a wealth of information. But is it really necessary for us to know about *all* the negative events taking place every day in the entire world? It *is* important to know about our local situation, it *is* important to know about our country's economic and political situation, it *is* important to know about the major events taking place across the world, but is it really necessary for us to know about every theft, rape, murder, kidnapping, abuse and tragedy happening on the other side of the planet? Steer clear from an unproductive overdose of negative information, also because by focusing on negative events that provoke negative emotions in you, you are running the risk of attracting them into your own personal reality and you are also preventing your desires from becoming a part of your life experience.

Are accidents accidental or do people attract them?

Accidents are not accidental. Accidents occur because:

- you established before coming into this physical plane of existence (your Life Project) to have an accident in order to learn from this experience and evolve spiritually;

OR

- you have attracted the accident into your life experience through your thoughts, words or deeds (like attracts like) or through your focused attention to someone or something.

When accidents take place with more than one person involved, each person attracted the event for one reason or another.

Is it easier to attract what I want through sacrifice and hard work?

Do the words "hard work", "sacrifice", "toil", "sweat" and "effort" seem appealing to you? Unless you're a masochist, they are not. These words describe actions that are far from pleasing, though we mistakenly believe that they are necessary to achieve our goals and succeed in life. But the truth is very simple: the easiest way to attract what you want in life is to be happy in your Here-and-Now.

Why is man perennially unsatisfied?

It is in our nature to have desires and aspirations. Once we satisfy a desire, we find ourselves in a new, different reality that causes a shift of our perspective. From this new viewpoint, we are confronted with - and pay attention to - new contrasts that will inspire us to formulate new desires. This is an eternal process that contributes towards the expansion of the Universe.

I have a big problem that I need to solve. What can help me?

If you have already tried to find a rational solution to your problem and have also asked others for help but haven't solved your problem yet, ask the Universe for guidance. Sit or lie in a quiet place, close your eyes and calm your mind (meditate) *without thinking of your problem*. One way is to think, as you inhale, of the air entering your nostrils and to think, as you exhale, of the air exiting your nostrils. Continue to do this for 10-15 minutes.

In addition to meditating, ask the Universe for help before falling asleep at night. Very often you will receive an intuition that will help you overcome your obstacle. If for some reason you do not, then turn your attention entirely away from your problem and focus your attention instead on anything that makes you feel good.

I have just entertained a negative thought. What should I do?

As soon as you realize that you are having a negative thought or feeling, you have the power to deliberately focus on another thought that makes you feel better. Therefore, rather than focusing on something that you don't want, turn your attention to something that you do want. This way, you will not only return to being aligned with your spiritual self but you will feel better and also prevent attracting negative circumstances or events into your future. Do not allow the negative thought or feeling to grow!

Are my continued negative thoughts harmful?

The physical world is the slowest thought-responsive plane of existence, so it takes more time for thoughts to translate into manifestations. This means that if you have a negative thought or feeling, you - fortunately - do not instantly create a negative circumstance or event in your life.

But if you continue to have negative thoughts, you can – and will – attract negative situations into your life. Persistent negative thoughts, such as "I'll never be able to..." or "the situation will never change", as well as persistent negative emotions, such as hate, jealousy and anger, will without fail bring negative circumstances or events into your personal life experience.

Why do I need to quiet my mind (meditate)?

The mind is the mediator between the physical body and the soul. It is easier for us to receive intuitions when we are completely relaxed and our minds are quiet. When we are in a meditative state, the door of the spiritual world is opened to us and we can pick up a very helpful intuition, a stroke of genius or inspiration.

I need to make some changes in my life but am having a hard time passing from thought to action. What should I do?

Action is imperative! Do you *watch* sports or do you *play* sports? Do you read novels or do you fall in love, have an adventure, climb a mountain?

In the physical world we live in, knowing or thinking something in your mind doesn't mean much at all until you have transmitted your knowledge or thought to someone else or you have turned the knowledge or thought into action. To get started in the action mode, write a list of the changes you want in your life. Then pinpoint which you consider is the most urgent change that needs to be addressed. Ask yourself: "What can I do *today* to improve this situation?" Do not think about *tomorrow* or *next week* or *next month*. Think only of *today*. Life is today and not tomorrow or next week or next month. Then turn off your tv and your pc, put your book down and go do it. Any action – even a tiny step in the direction of your objective – is better than no action at all. And smile! The next morning, and every morning, again ask yourself what is most urgent and then write what you can do *today* and *go do it.*

I feel stressed out and don't have enough time to do everything I should or want to do. What should I do?

When you feel stressed out and that you lack the time to do everything your want to or should do, not only will you attract more stressful situations, but you are preventing yourself from receiving the circumstances and events that you have asked for. You should therefore press the "hold" button and realize that you can only do one thing well at a time. Multitasking is counterproductive and can be dangerous, such as driving and talking on the phone or texting at the same time. Being in the Here-and-Now means being fully present with your mind and your heart every single moment of the day. It means being conscious, being aware of the people, the circumstances and events in your life, rather than seeing everything as one massive hectic blur. You have the power to stop and calmly, lovingly do one thing at a time.

Which emotions indicate that it's time for me to stop doing something?

If you are doing something unwillingly or if you feel uncomfortable or bored doing something - whether it's a relationship or a job or what you previously considered a fun hobby - you should reflect on whether it's time to make some changes in your life.

Why are there lucky and unlucky people in the world?

There is no such thing as chance or fate. It is our beliefs and expectations, our focused thoughts and intentions, combined with emotion, that create and shape our personal reality. We in fact co-create our personal reality through our thoughts, words or deeds (like attracts like), through our focused attention to someone or something or because we decided in advance to experience certain circumstances or events (Life Project).

> *In July 2017 I went to a park with my granddaughter Eleonora and I told her, "I always find coins and precious things!" We stayed in the park for an hour and a half and as were going back towards the car I found an antique coin on the ground that was about 200 years old. It was my belief and expectation that led me to find the coin that no one else had seen in all those years.*

How can I help someone who is unhappy?

The only way that someone can be happy is for him or her to *decide* to be happy. We can however help the person realize that we are co-creators of our personal life experience and that through our words, actions, thoughts and emotions, we emit a corresponding vibration into the Universe and end up attracting our rewards and our punishments as a magnet attracts iron. We can tell the person that they can stop attracting negative people and events and instead start consciously/intentionally attracting positive people and events into their personal reality. Through focused thought combined with emotion, they can - and will -

65

attract the vibrational match of what they are emanating.

We can offer our advice, we can help the person by visualizing him/her as happy, we can encourage the person to change his/her ways, we can set a good example, and we can offer our love but there is nothing more that we can do. Every woman and every man is the architect of her/his own life and it is up to her/him to decide to change, as each person is gifted with free will.

Do objects retain the energy of the person they have been in contact with?

Every object retains the energy of who made it – from the cooked food that you eat, to the furniture in your house, to the paintings on your walls...

Objects can be intentionally charged with negative energy – obviously by people who are spiritually deprived.

Psychometry is the ability to know something about the past owner of an object simply by touching the object.

My Reiki teacher Massimo Ballestrazzi has an interesting psychometry story to tell:

The psychometry experience that struck me the most happened years ago during a mediumship seminar. I was given a box containing an object and I had to describe what I saw and felt, just like the other participants. This was one of the first times that I had done something like this and I didn't know exactly what to do. I just closed my eyes and as soon as I did I began to see images flashing by right in front of me. I looked on as if it were a film. When the exercise was over, one by one the participants spoke about what they had experienced and established if there was any relevance between those experiences and the object in the box. When it was my turn (and I still laugh when I think about it), I said that I hadn't seen anything in particular. Just a sort of movie. And then I described what I had seen...

Initially a light blue vortex that opened onto a field. A blond woman whose face I don't see gets off a white car. I knew however that she wore glasses. The woman was walking towards a country house. The funny thing was that while she was approaching the house, she became increasingly younger and the house became increasingly older, until she became a child. She was riding a red bicycle with white handlebars in the courtyard and she was happy. I knew though that she felt sad now. She was wearing red sandals, the types with little holes at the front. Then I saw two adults who were playing with her and hugging her tight. In the here and now, I knew that the blond woman missed those people and felt unhappy. The last image was a kidney. To make it short, there was a car key in the box and it belonged to a blond woman in our group who wore glasses. I described a moment of her life when she was a child at her grandparents' home and the bike that was waiting for her there every time she went to visit them.

I asked Massimo if there was any connection with the kidney he had seen. He replied: *She told me that in the past she had had some renal colics and that she no longer had them. I hadn't given much thought at the time to the kidney as I was focusing on all the rest. It was as if this last image was additional proof to give her.*

What can prevent me from meeting my goals in life?

The following prevent you from reaching our goals:

1. Your negative thoughts, emotions, words and deeds.
2. Lack of confidence in yourself.
3. Weak desire to achieve your goal.
4. Giving up too soon.
5. Not passing from thought to action, perhaps owing to indecisiveness.

Action is imperative! Ask yourself: "What can I do *today* to reach my goal?" Do not think about *tomorrow* or *next week* or *next month*. Think only of *today*. Life is today and not tomorrow or next week or next month. Then do it. Any action – even a tiny step in the direction of your objective – is better than no action at all. That said, if you are *very* hesitant as which course of action to take, sometimes it's better to stay still and things may work out on their own. As with all things, be very attentive as to your emotions. Do only what you feel good doing and avoid all other actions.

What is déjà vu?

Déjà vu is the odd feeling that you have experienced the very same situation before. It may be that you have in fact experienced the very same situation before – not in this lifetime but in a previous life experience.

What can forcibly shake me into re-establishing my priorities in life?

Earthquakes and other disasters can help us instantaneously appreciate once again the true value of all that we have, beginning with our family and friends, and instantly eliminates all unnecessary distractions. But let's not wait for a calamity to take place and let's instead learn to recognize and be grateful for what we have and put our priorities in the right order.

Which special individual power can help me change my reality?

Gratitude is the key to evolving spiritually and to changing our reality. It opens our heart to the splendor of life.

Write down in a notebook all the reasons you are deeply grateful for what you are or have. Do this every day for a week – you will see that you will discover more and more reasons every day for which to be grateful. You will also see that so much more abundance will come your way as a result. By opening your heart this way, you will attract increasingly more circumstances and events to be grateful for.

Another powerful way to change your reality is to find the connection between you and the rest of humanity. Take a walk, observe others, enter into empathy with them, open your eyes and your heart to the beauty that surrounds you.

What can help me if I don't believe in myself – that is, if I limit what I can be and do?

Sit in a quiet place, close your eyes and calm your mind (for example, use a meditation method or count mentally). After about 10 minutes, gently open your eyes and write down on a piece of paper what you would do in your life if you had no limits, if you weren't afraid of failing. Let your imagination go wild! And - for as long as possible - hold on to the emotions you feel of the freedom of being and doing whatever you want. By doing this, you will gradually remove dubious thoughts of self-worth and begin to make your dreams come true.

Can I read someone's mind?

You can, but the other person must be on your same wavelength.

In January 2017, I went to a Laboratory of Invisible Perceptions conducted by Massimo Ballestrazzi. After a guided meditation and various extrasensorial experiments, I was instructed to sit before a young man, Davide, who I had never met before, and to try to read each other's thoughts. We sat facing each other. My hands were palms up, if I remember well, while his were above mine palms down. I suggested to Davide to narrow our thoughts to an animal. We both closed our eyes and I immediately saw some water and a dolphin's nose appear and I told him what I had seen. Davide seemed very surprised and told me that yes, he had thought about a dolphin. He was thinking about when he was four years old. He had gone with his grandparents to an aquatic park and he had been chosen to feed the dolphins! He asked me if I had seen other details but I told him that all I had seen was the water and the dolphin. I believe that I was able to pick up his thought not only because he was transmitting this thought to me, but also because this thought of his had an emotional content.

Can I predict a future event?

You definitely have the faculty of predicting future events, but you need to develop this power by practicing, just like you would do to learn a new language. Some people are able to predict future events from information received through their dreams or when they are in a meditative state. When you begin to "know" that this is possible, you will be able to predict more and more future events.

Very late one night in January 1981 I was returning from Bologna to Minerbio where I lived. In the car, I began thinking about my cat Juvia. Juvia was an extraordinary cat. She was almost human. She walked beside me without a leash in the middle of the city, she played hide-and-go-seek with me, she knew when I was feeling happy or sad... I loved her very much as she did me. In the car, I thought, "Juvia is dead". I don't know why but I immediately did the superstitious gesture that they do in Italy called the "corna" (you extend your forefinger and little finger while holding on to your middle and ring finger with your thumb). This is supposed to prevent the bad thing you are thinking about from happening. After a while, though, I noticed that I had forgotten to keep my hands in this position and I remember thinking, "Now there is nothing I can do." A few meters later we found Juvia dead in the middle of the street.

*****

In the early morning of 6 April 2009 I dreamt I was in a house where the walls had enormous veins (like the veins on my hand) that were swelling up. It seemed to me like the water pipes in the walls were about to explode. I yelled to my husband, who was in the shower, "Run, the house is about to explode!" He however didn't hear me. My son

Federico was with me along with another child and I told them to put on their shoes and run out.
When I woke up, I found out that there had been a terrible earthquake in L'Aquila at 3:32 a.m., leaving over 250 dead, many hurt and missing.

PHYSICAL AND MENTAL HEALTH

What does pain mean?

Pain is the physical indication that we <u>urgently</u> need to change something in our life. At first it's the negative emotions we feel that signal we have to change something in our life. If we continue to ignore those negative feelings for a long time, then our body steps in, making us feel pain. Our body's intent is to force us to stop and analyze what is going on in our lives and to make the necessary changes, whether this means turning our thoughts, words or deeds from negative to positive ones or focusing our attention to someone or something that is wanted rather than unwanted.

Why do people become ill?

The reason we experience negative circumstances or events - including diseases - is that we have invited them into our life experience through:

- *our continued negative thoughts, words or actions (Law of Vibrational Attraction)*

Everything in the Universe produces an energetic vibration and our words, actions, and even our emotions and thoughts (the *cause*) have a consequence (the *effect*), whether we do so intentionally or unintentionally. Vibrations of the same frequency attract each other (like attracts like), which means that if we are kind we will attract a person, situation or event into our personal reality that is a vibrational match to kindness. It is we who attract our rewards and our punishments through our words, actions, thoughts and feelings, somewhat like a magnet attracts iron. Once we realize that we attract the corresponding effect of our words, actions, thoughts and feelings, we can stop attracting negative people and events and instead start consciously/intentionally attracting positive people and events - including good health - into our personal reality;

- *our continued attention to a circumstance or event (Law of Focused Thought Manifestation)*

When we *repeatedly* turn our attention to a circumstance or event, we end up attracting it (or something very similar to it) into our own experience, whether we desire it or not. For example, by thinking consistently with deep emotion about another person who is suffering from a disease, or about poverty, about immigration invasion, about burglaries... we end up attracting the relative situation (or something very similar to it) into our own experience;

- *a lesson to learn that we pre-established before being born (our Life Project)*

Before coming into the physical world, each of us pre-established certain life lessons or events in our lifetime as an opportunity to experience, learn from and spiritually evolve from these. So these pre-established events - which may be based on lessons that we failed to learn in previous lives or new challenges we wanted to experience - take place at some point of our lifetime. It could be, for example, that we choose to have a certain disease and that the plan involves our getting a genetic disease from one of our relatives. The contrasts and situations we experience provoke desires, which we are able to turn into manifestations through our positive thoughts, words and deeds, as well as through focused thought combined with emotion. Our pre-established contrasts force us to grow and learn;

- *a drop in energy (excessive physical or mental stress)*

When we overdo things – pushing our body to work more and more, to exercise more and more, to run around trying to do more and more for others – our body sends out a signal telling us that it's time for us to sit down and get back our energy and life. If a drop in energy is what caused you to become ill, in most cases rest as well as identifying and deciding to respect your hierarchy of life values will help you to re-establish good health. Reiki treatments can also be of great help if your energy level has dropped.

Having the gift of free will, we are free at any time to change our personal reality, whatever is the cause of our negative experience.

Do babies also attract illness?
Children and even babies are no different than adults are, though they are much less likely to attract illness through continued negative thoughts, words or actions compared to adults.

Can you inherit a disease from a relative?
Not through your genes, unless the disease was a circumstance that you pre-established before coming into your physical body. Otherwise you attract diseases – as anything else that is negative – through their continued negative thoughts, words or actions or by giving your focused attention to someone or something that is negative.

I am ill. What should I do first of all?

Evaluate whether you have attracted your illness into your reality through your continued negative thoughts, words or actions *(Law of Vibrational Attraction)* or your continued attention to a circumstance or event *(Law of Focused Thought Manifestation)*. Think back to when the first symptoms of your illness appeared. What were you doing then? What were your thoughts at that time? What were you doing and saying? Were you happy? Did you want for something to change in your life? If you find that it is possible for you to have manifested your illness through one of these two laws, you can start intentionally attracting good health into your personal reality (see the *Wish Come True Technique on page 41*). Also remember that the cells of our body are intelligent and that most of them naturally regenerate over time.

So turn your thoughts away from all that is unwanted, including your disease, and start creating your new healthy life <u>now</u>. Start by not thinking yourself as ill. Say "I am healthy" aloud, repeat it and totally believe it. You are a powerful divine being. The things you say mold your reality so either talk of good health or say nothing at all. Do not make the mistake of speaking to others of your illness, which will only propagate your condition... Remember to erase the word "sickness" from your vocabulary.

If you lack faith in your power, then ask the Creator, a saint or other spiritual helper who you totally believe in... The important thing is faith. Faith performs miracles.

> *Sit or lie in a quiet place, close your eyes and calm your mind (meditate) without thinking of your problem. One way is to think, as you inhale, of the air entering your nostrils and to think, as you exhale, of the air exiting your nostrils. Continue to do this for 10-15 minutes. In addition to meditating, ask the Universe for help before falling asleep at night. Very often you will receive an intuition that will help you overcome your obstacle. If for some reason you do not, then turn your attention entirely away from your problem and focus your attention instead on anything that makes you feel good.*

Which conditions can prevent me from being healthy?

1. *Allowing your energy level to drop*

Physical and mental stress (from arguing with someone in the office to overdoing it in the gym) cause your energy level to drop. Rest, meditation or other techniques, such as Reiki, can easily bring your energy level back up if you immediately recognize that you are in a state of physical or mental stress. So set your limits, don't overdo it, learn to say "no" and be mindful about how you feel. If you don't, the initial drop of energy can lead to your feeling worse and worse and you can end up sick and/or depressed.

2. *Eating foods and beverages that we know are not nourishing (what you believe is bad for you is bad for you) or not consuming enough foods that we know that are nourishing.*

If we were truly in harmony with Who We Really Are, foods would however be unnecessary - and we wouldn't lose a single ounce - as we could obtain all the energy we require from the Universe. Remember

77

that foods, along with every other thing in the world, have vibrational frequencies. For this reason, foods that have been processed without ethics should be avoided.

3. *Lack of physical exercise*
4. *Abuse of caffeine, sugar, tobacco, alcohol, recreational drugs and medicinal drugs*
5. *Your negative thoughts, emotions, words and actions*
6. *Your focused attention to a negative circumstance or event*
7. *Toxic environments*

For example, places that make you feel ill at ease, places where there is a lot of noise, too much or too little light, lack of fresh air, too much heating, too much air conditioning. Any place you consider unhealthy or bad for you is unhealthy or bad for you.

8. *Contact with negative people - that is, with people who think, say and do negative things*

What are the keys to optimal physical and mental health?

1. *Follow a healthy diet based on fruit, vegetables and proteins (preferably vegetarian proteins);*
2. *Do physical exercise:* minimum of 30 minute walk per day in the fresh air;
3. *Open your heart.*
   Let go of your negative emotions and turn your thoughts, words and deeds into positive ones;
4. *Hang out with virtuous, positive people – people who think, say and do positive things;*
5. *Stay in clean positive environments;*
6. *Do anything to keep your vibrations high: smile, be thankful, be filled with wonder, love;*

7. *Be extra careful of your emotions*, which will always help you to understand what's good for you and what isn't;

8. *Make sure your energy centers (chakras) are spinning properly* - through meditation, Reiki and other practices.

I am worrying about the future. What should I do?

Forget the future and ask yourself: " What can I do *today/now* to improve my life?" Do not think about *tomorrow* or *next week* or *next month*. Think only of *today* and *now*. Life is *now* and not tomorrow or next week or next month. Then take action.

Any action – even a tiny step in the direction of your objective – is better than no action at all. A good start is to open your heart and smile, be kind to yourself and to others.

How does the spiritual healing process take place?

We become physically ill because we in some way have distanced ourselves from Who We Really Are – that is, divine sparks. In most cases, we attract illness through our continued negative thoughts, words or actions *(Law of Vibrational Attraction)* or through our continued attention to a negative circumstance or event *(Law of Focused Thought Manifestation)*. When we are ill, our natural energy is depleted – and we no longer know how to access the unlimited energy of the Universe that can make us feel better again. Spiritual healers, such as qualified Reiki practitioners, can help those who have lost touch with their true essence to re-establish contact with their spiritual selves, so that they can restore their innate self-healing power.

I am nervous and upset. What should I do?
To re-establish your natural state of mental wellbeing, you must turn your thoughts away from what has made you nervous or upset. You can:

- empty your mind through meditation (see page 238 – "How can I meditate?");

- distract your mind: watch an amusing film, take a walk in nature, listen to music, read a book, do physical exercises, tend to your flowers, do a crossword puzzle, a sudoku, or do anything else that is pleasing to you.

Only when you are calm and relaxed again can you analyze the situation objectively. What made you nervous or upset and why? In most cases, it's our reaction to things happening that needs to be readjusted. Sit down and write about what led you to react the way you did and what you can do to avoid feeling the same way again.

What should parents who have children born with disabilities know?
All children born - with or without disabilities - are divine sparks and powerful co-creators of their life experience. Before coming into this physical plane of existence, children born with disabilities established in their Life Project to have an infirmity. Moreover, the parents of disabled children accepted and wanted to have this family role in their Life Project. Choosing to be a parent of a child with a disability may seem incredible and absurd at first, but since it's the closest of all types of relationships, it has an amazing potential for spiritual growth, not only for the child but also for the parents. Our life experiences are precious

learning lessons so that we can ultimately acquire the qualities of an evolved soul: love, compassion, kindness, gratitude, joy...

I am ill and traditional medicine is not helping me. What can I do?

First make sure that you follow all steps listed on page 78: "What are the keys to optimal physical and mental health?".

You may *also* (but not *only*) try one of the following holistic practices, which will help you to unblock your energy:

- *Reiki*
- *Acupuncture*
- *Reflexology*
- *Ayurvedic Medicine*
- *Chiropractic*
- *ThetaHealing®*
- *Tai chi*
- *Qigong*
- *Hatha Yoga*
- *Kriya Yoga*
- *Ashtanga Yoga*
- *Family Constellations*
- *Osteopathy with cranialsacral technique*
- *Past-Life Regression* (See page 182: "How can I find out about my previous life/lives? and page 186: "Is it useful to have a past-life regression?").

Whatever you choose to try, make sure you turn to a qualified and experienced practitioner. Stay away from those who charge enormous sums of money. A true spiritual healer is one who would do it for free but charges the amount required to live decently.

The doctors say that I cannot be healed. Should I believe them?

If the doctors tell you that you cannot be cured, be aware of the fact that this is simply their belief, based on their limited knowledge of the human being, who is not just flesh and bones but much much more... The important thing is that *you want, believe and expect* that you can become healthy again. You can decide to be healthy. Think of yourself as already healed. Have unshakable faith in your mind that you are healthy.

Can I heal without traditional medicine?

At a late stage, some ailments necessarily require traditional medicine, such as the dentist, who cures your cavities, or the orthopedic, who puts your broken leg in a cast so that it can heal properly, or the surgeon, who removes your tumor. Holistic practices - such as Reiki, ThetaHealing® and acupuncture - can however help you to avoid getting to the point that you need a dentist, an orthopedic or a surgeon. When we become ill or have an accident, our body is trying to tell us something: that we need to slow down, that we need to change something in our life that is causing us grief, anger, sadness or that we need to change the way we are reacting to certain circumstances and events of our life. If we continue to disregard those signals that our body is sending out - such as pain, feeling tired or stressed, becoming too skinny or too fat – we will definitely develop a physical disorder that could be life-threatening. Holistic therapies put you into contact with your spiritual self and set off your innate self-healing process. You must however pay extreme attention to your emotions, thoughts, words and deeds, and change what needs to be changed in your life, so that you can return to being happy and healthy.

How can I break a bad habit?
A bad habit is anything that you do repeatedly that is undesirable to yourself and/or to others. You are a divine spark and a powerful co-creator so don't for a minute think that you can't break your bad habit, because you can. Follow the *Wish Come True Technique* (see page 41) to the letter and your bad habit will vanish. Say "NO" to your bad habit, steer clear from the people and places that instigate or tempt you. Raise your vibrational frequency and remember that you are much more than your five physical senses. Do not allow yourself to be a slave to any of your physical senses.

Use the following technique to help you get through a temptation or crisis moment:

BREATHING TECHNIQUE TO HELP OVERCOME BAD HABIT CRISIS MOMENTS
Close your eyes and focus on your breathing, inhaling and exhaling as if you were smoking a cigarette. It's not a coincidence that we start our physical lives by breathing and we end it with our last breath. It's not a coincidence that so many people in the world were and are addicted to smoking cigarettes. Focused breath control opens the door to the spiritual world. Take a deep breath through your nose while mentally counting up to 3, hold your breath for 3 seconds and then slowly

exhale through your mouth for 4-8 seconds. Continue smoking your smoke-free cigarette for 3-5 minutes, which is the time it usually takes to smoke a real cigarette. Smoke your virtual cigarettes at different points of the day, especially when you feel tense or have any other negative emotion.

What can be done to help someone else overcome his/her addiction to drugs or alcohol?

Those who are addicted to drugs or who are dependent on alcohol are attempting to smother the emotion of fear and insecurity they feel. Each person is a divine spark and 100% responsible for his/her own life. By numbing or otherwise altering the emotions they feel, which are true indicators of where they are in relation to their spiritual essences and also reveal whether they are aligned or not with their desires, they are trying to dodge their responsibilities. They are denying the fact of being powerful co-creators of their life experience. They are blaming drugs and alcohol for their not being the person that they want to be – that is their weak excuse. How can we help a loved one who has placed himself/herself in this awful situation? We can offer our advice, we can encourage the person to change his/her ways, we can set a good example, and we can offer our love but there is nothing more that we can do. Every woman and every man is the architect of her/his own life and it is up to her/him to decide to change, as each person is gifted with free will. Who are we to prevent free will? Do continue to sincerely love this person whether he or she takes or does not take the decision to quit drugs or alcohol. Please note however that loving doesn't mean your having to live with someone else's bad decisions and bad habits, also because your continued attention to these undesirable events could lead to your attracting undesirable events into your own life experience.

I am overweight. What should I do?

If you are already aware of what a healthy diet should be but are fat nonetheless, it means that you have focused your thoughts on being fat.

Most people with weight problems overeat, which means ingesting more calories (energy) than your body requires.

The reasons that people overeat vary:

- *Feeling of insecurity* – that is, the subconscious fear of being deprived of the necessary calories to survive.

  If this is your issue, past-life regression hypnosis could be beneficial, as well as Reiki, ThetaHealing®, meditation and other holistic therapies.

- *Hedonism* – that is, self-indulging in the sensorial pleasures of food. If this is what triggers your eating lots more than you should, you can try to pay less and less attention to physical, materialistic aspects and more and more attention to spiritual aspects. The physical senses are great to have but too much attention to these can enslave us and keep us from evolving.

- *Unresolved past trauma*

  In this case, ThetaHealing®, meditation, family constellations, past-life regression hypnosis and emotional healing therapies can be of great help.

- *Not living in the present* - that is, thinking about something else while you're eating, such as thinking about what you have to do after eating, or thinking about the next food you want to eat without paying attention or enjoying what you're doing at the present moment. By living in the Here-and-Now, you can instead pick up the messages that your body is sending you, informing you that the food that you're eating is not good for you or that you've already ingested enough calories.

The fat that you accumulate when you overeat is simply stored energy that needs to be transformed into useful energy. Is it easier for you to burn fat through physical exertion or is it easier for you to eat less? That's yours to decide.

What should parents do when their children are sick?

We parents have an extraordinary task, which we are not always so great at performing: being an example of kindness, of balance and love to our children. Our life example - that is, our words and actions - are crucial to our children's happiness and health. We first need to get in tune with Who We Really Are to be able to help our children when they are sick or at any time of need. We need to make sure we have an open heart and do and say things that are in harmony with our true divine essence.

Let's avoid for our children to get sick in the first place by:

- making sure our home be a clean, positive environment – a place where our child can grow with other family members who think, say and do positive, loving things;

  - making sure they have a balanced, healthy diet based on fruit, vegetables and proteins;

  - encouraging our children to do some physical exercise - nothing forcible but just what they *enjoy* doing. They could for example have fun at the playground or play ping pong, dance to music, swim or take a walk in the park, with the excuse of finding beautiful autumn leaves...;

  - making sure our children get the right amount of sleep – not too much and not too little, depending on our children's age;

  - teaching our children to pay attention to their emotions (see page 37: "Why do I need to pay extreme attention to my emotions?").

When your children are sick, wrap them in love and try to find out what made them become sick. Sometimes, it's because they are overwhelmed with studying or other activities and they simply need to rest and recover their energy to be well again.

Where is the soul of a person in a coma?
While the physical body of a person in a coma seems inanimate, its spirit (along with its soul) is very much alive. It is in the astral world for the most part, where it reviews and analyzes its current lifetime and decides whether or not to return to the physical world.

How can I attempt to awaken someone who is in a coma?

Ensitiv, Italy's astral travel expert, has developed a technique to assist those who have loved ones in a coma.

PROTOCOL NO. 1 ENSITIV METHOD
The Soul and Awakening from Coma
(Synthesis extracted from the book "Viaggiatore Astrale" by Ensitiv)

Soul energy is capable of feeling and hearing the most especially when the body's functions are reduced. Unfortunately, as I have often repeated, the two worlds - the spiritual/material world and the exclusively energetic world - have completely different forms of communication. (...)

There are however techniques that can be used to increase the possibility of being perceived/heard and especially to spur the Soul to gather and retrieve the energy needed to overcome the shortcomings of the body and restore eventual physical and brain damage. (...)

Following my research and as I explained in "Manuale per Sopravvivere dopo la Morte" (Guide to Surviving after Death), when the mind pays less attention to the material and physical environment, the Soul definitely separates from the body - not because of death, but owing to the simple phenomenon of entering the Astral Dimension with a double body or an OBE, a sort of near-death experience.

What actually happens in a comatose state is: the body lies helpless on a bed, often kept alive by mechanical means, while the Soul is separated from its material part for most of the day and hovers between the real dimension and the astral dimension as if it were having a long dream from which it couldn't wake up.

(...) we see that those in the energetic world have the ability to hear and comprehend stimuli, therefore what we have to do is to try to find the right frequency and the right message.

As in any dream, the messages that get through are those repeated with a warm and convincing tone. The message, which must always be positive and an incentive to "returning" or "awakening", must be repeated constantly. A confident voice, familiar words and repeated out loud, but not aggressively.

The name of the person should be pronounced clearly in each message and objects and things with which the person has a special bond can be used as a catalyst. I suggest making these attempts at different moments of the day and motivating the Soul to restore its physical function by providing it also, where possible, with adequate electromagnetic energy. A constant source of free energy, such as a battery placed near the individual, can be of great help if the Soul's resources have weakened.

I am convinced that the use of plants, animals or crystals greatly helps the "spirit" to focus its attention on the message being transmitted by the person's loved ones. (...)

If possible, a sort of "opening theme song" should be used before each message. It can be the sound of an alarm clock, the verse of a song that the individual particularly likes, the ring of a mobile phone or anything that would have usually aroused his/her attention. (...) as soon as the "theme song" finishes, pronounce the name of the person several times as if you were wakening him/her from sleep and constantly request his/her participation in restoring his/her vital functions. In these moments, leave out the tears and despair, which are of little use. Give way to optimism and endeavor to arouse a feeling of confidence and positivity.

An Energy separated from its body receives the sounds

coming from the Real Dimension as if they were coming in through water, since there is a big difference in densities. Consequently, complex messages, stories or requesting answers are useless. (...)

Theme song, Name, Catalyzing objects and constant and firmly repeated Messages should be attempted every day, taking note of the slightest reaction. (...)

If you have planned to spend one or more hours at the bedside of your loved one, do not do it in silence and don't talk about how you spent your day. Do it using the method set out in these notes. If you decide to use music, CHANGE THE HZ FREQUENCY and take note of the eventual reactions to every change.

If you use a Catalyzing Object, do not let it lay still on the nightstand, but move it when you are "transmitting" your message.

If you use a "theme song", do not wait too long before talking to him/her. (...)

Using constant SOURCES OF LIGHT can be helpful. Candles are fine as long as you light them right before you call the person. Or use flashlights that have a different light from the one in the room and switch them on and off at regular intervals. You should never however place them far from you. (...)

http://ensitiv.blogspot.com

How can I get rid of my anxiety/fear?

We need to be fearful only of things that are truly - and not hypothetically - endangering to our body or mind. If you have irrational fears, the only way to rid yourself of them is to face them. You can practice confronting - and winning - your fear in your mind. So if you are fearful of flying, imagine yourself getting on an airplane and arriving safely to your destination; if you dread the very thought of a certain animal, imagine yourself seeing it and smoothly walking by; if you are afraid of heights, imagine yourself climbing to the top of the Empire State Building and looking with interest at the view of New York City; if you are in the habit of expecting yourself to be robbed every time you take a walk downtown, imagine yourself relishing your stroll and picture yourself getting back home with your wallet. Some of us are used to imagining all the most dreadful things happening to us, as if we wanted to prepare ourselves for the worst that can happen in case it does happen... But the truth is that fears are unproductive. They are just negative thoughts that we have that cause us to live unhappily. With a bit of practice and a little sense of humor, we can change our fearful thoughts into fearless or at least neutral/indifferent ones.

What are so-called night terrors (pavor nocturnus) and what are they caused by?

Pavor nocturnus - also called night terror - is a frightening state that happens during sleep. This condition is more commonly experienced by children than by adults. The sleeping child suddenly sits up in bed and begins screaming, pointing and talking to people that others cannot see. The child is terrified, his/her eyes are closed or half closed and it's very difficult to soothe him/her. He/she has no recollection of the event upon waking. Pavor nocturnus is not a nightmare. It is actually a spontaneous out-of-body experience induced by having done strenuous physical activities (running, jumping, swimming...) shortly prior to sleep. The phenomena connected to out-of-body experiences – such as intense body vibrations,

91

unusual sounds and body paralysis – can be indeed frightening for a child and in this terror-stricken state the child can attract undesirable entities in the astral plane.

How can I help a child to overcome fear during so-called night terrors?

If your child is prone to having episodes of pavor nocturnus, first of all make sure he doesn't do too much physical activity before going to bed. Do not deny or ignore what your child says he/she dreams, sees or feels. The child should be made to understand that there is nothing bad or wrong, everything he has experienced is part of the natural world. Also explain to your child that it's very important to stay calm and that in any case no one can physically hurt him. A mischievous entity in the astral world is not so different from a mosquito in the physical world. Your child should know that his spirit guide is always there by his side and that in order to get support and comfort all he has to do is to ask. Inform your child that if he feels his body jolt, shake or vibrate or if he hears strange sounds, he should think about a specific part of his body – his foot for example. By the simple fact of thinking about your physical body, you return to your physical body, thereby ending the OBE.

I am unhappy. Why should I then ignore (rather than pay attention to) my current reality?

If are unhappy and you continue to pay attention to your current reality, wallowing in your unhappiness, there is no way that you can change your situation. Remember that all circumstances and events in our lives have been put there by our individual selves and by no one else. We however have the power of changing our negative situation at any time by refusing to give it our focused attention. The only way to change your current reality is to raise your vibrations and to find a way to accept the situation instead of fighting it. By doing so, the unhappy situation will dissolve on its own. Rather than thinking about your current state, concentrate instead on creating the future that you desire (see the *Wish Come True Technique on page 41*).

How can I help someone who is ill?

Help the person to turn his/her attention away from the illness and to focus instead on positive thoughts, circumstances and events. Your paying considerable attention to someone else's illness not only hinders the person from healing but also attracts illness into your own personal reality. People who are ill tend to speak constantly about their illness and by doing so they are perpetuating the illness. Listening to them speak about their illness may seem a polite and sympathetic thing for you to do but it actually does no one any good. So help them instead to divert their negative thoughts and to entertain happy thoughts even if for a short time (point out the beautiful sunset that is painting the horizon, talk about a funny thing that happened at work, tell the person something nice - that her eyes/hair/dress looks great today...).

Something else you can do to help is to visualize your friend or relative in your mind, like a film. Imagine the person in good health and feel the emotion and the joy that this scene provokes in you, then try to keep this emotion for as long as you can.

What can speed up the aging process?

Our physical body was projected to last a lot longer than 100 years but our current limited beliefs and thoughts usually lead us to age and die prior to reaching 100. If you believe that you are getting old, you will. If you lose interest in life, that will also speed up your aging process. Because your reality is based on your thoughts, intentions, beliefs and expectations.

What can slow down the aging process?

If you are full of interests and wanting to learn and share and love, then your physical aging process will slow down. *Feeling* young also slows down the process. Having lived on planet Earth for more years than other people doesn't mean decadence but signifies more experience, more wisdom, more opportunity for learning and growth, more opportunity for sharing and loving and caring...

When you see yourself reflected in the mirror in the morning, tell yourself: "My body and my mind are ageless. I transcend time. Every cell of my body is flooded by light, energy and love."

Why is sleep so important?

Sleep recharges our body's energy, just like electricity recharges batteries. A part of our consciousness though stays in our physical body during sleep so that our body functions continue to operate.

The dreams we have provide us with the key to solve the problems that we haven't been able to solve with our conscious mind. Dreams also give us feedback on where we are currently at and on what we are attracting into our life experience.

Do we co-create our personal reality also when we sleep?

The creative and spiritual part of us - our soul - leaves our physical body when we sleep. We therefore do not attract circumstances and events into our life experience during sleep.

What is the right amount of sleep for an adult?

Eight hours of sleep is the norm for adults, though some people require less hours of sleep (6-7 hours) and others need more hours (9-10) to feel refreshed and full of energy. Lack of the right amount of sleep may cause you to be irritable or depressed. On the other hand, when you sleep too much, the body loses its muscle tone and you wake up feeling tired rather than refreshed.

What can I do if I suffer from insomnia?

Begin by relaxing all parts of your body, starting from your feet. Say in your mind: "My feet are relaxed and heavy. My legs are relaxed and heavy." And slowly work your way up to your head, while loosening up muscle by muscle.

Counting (not necessarily sheep) is also useful for some people.

Repeating a mantra (a word or phrase of your choice) until you fall asleep is of great help to many.

WORK

What are the three steps towards professional success?

- *Do something that you enjoy doing*

If you choose a job that you do not enjoy doing, you are doing a disservice to yourself – because you are depriving yourself of joy for a good part of your life. Those who bend their heads and passively succumb to working day after day, year after year, in gray jobs they loathe can only attract equally unhappy events into their lives. Moreover, it is difficult to offer a good product or service if you don't put passion in your work.

Therefore, be careful to choose a job that you enjoy doing and while you are working, live in the moment by being fully concentrated on what you are doing.

- *Do something that is of value to others*

Choose a job that will help others in some way. Choose a product or service that is useful, ethical and environment friendly. Ask yourself "What is *my* contribution to humanity?"

- *Specialize and continue to improve*

Endeavor to become an expert in your field, by learning more and more and by sitting down to think and letting your imagination fly. Endeavor to go *beyond* what others have before you. *Know* and *feel* that you are a person of success. Be aware – leaving no room for doubt – that you are successful, period. Then apply what you have learned and dreamed up to your product or service.

I do not have the faintest clue of what I would like to do as a job. What should I do?

If you are uncertain about what you'd like to do as a job, the worst thing you can do is to listen to others. Others will tell you their thoughts, believing themselves to be helpful, but those thoughts are based on what *they* like to do. Do you want to live *your* life or *someone else's* life? Another bad choice is to select a career just because it's a type of job that others look at with respect... or just because you could earn lots of money... So many hours of our day are devoted to work, so let's try to avoid those jobs that we know right from the start that we would detest. Because our life isn't just "after work" – our life is every minute of the day, including the hours "at work", where we interact with others and express our individual essences.

So instead ask yourself:

- *What am I good at doing? Which are my talents?*

- *What would I enjoy doing that could be of benefit to others?*

If you continue to feel "stuck" and without ideas, pray for help in identifying a type of job where you can express your full potential. Ask the Universe to deliver the perfect job for you on a silver platter and have absolute, unshakable faith that the job will arrive. Before going to sleep, imagine yourself delighted about your new job... Feel yourself being proud, useful and truly satisfied for the wonderful new job that is about to arrive. Have faith that you will soon receive

97

an inspiration. Then take steps towards pursuing your heart's career.

That said, life is long and you may begin with one career and then evolve into a totally different scenario, because the world and market needs change in time and so do your interests.

The product/service I offer is a good one but I am having a hard time selling it. What should I do?

If you already know about the marketing mix - Product, Placement, Price and Promotion - and are absolutely certain that you haven't neglected one of the four P's but you still have difficulty in selling your product or service, you should analyze what is your point of attraction and those of your collaborators. Are you and they more concentrated on not having or on having? Are your and their thoughts, words and deeds positive ones? Is your and their heart in what you/they are doing or are you/they yearning to do something fresh and new? If you and your collaborators do have passion for what you are doing and your thoughts, words and actions are positive ones - not just on the job but at home and elsewhere – there is no reason that you should not be successful in selling what you are offering to others. Never ever talk about failure. Be very careful about the way you talk, as every word is like a magnet... If others ask you how things are going and you say that they're going bad, you are consolidating that reality.

To see which practical steps you can take, go to page 41 for the *Wish Come True Technique*.

I don't like my job. What should I do?

If you no longer like your job or if you never have right from the start, now is a good time to change it. That doesn't mean quitting today but it does mean taking a step *today* towards changing your situation. So take the time to think about what you would instead prefer to be doing, where and with who, and then take immediate action. Any action – even a tiny step in the direction of your objective – is better than no action at all. Life is Now, so don't waste it by spending so much of your time in a job that you detest.

I like my job but I have problems with my boss or with colleagues. What should I do?

Everyone who is a part of your life has been invited into your reality by you and you alone. You have attracted these people either because you are vibrating at the same frequency as they are (like attracts like) or because there is something that you need to learn from them before going forward. You should therefore stop and ponder whether you are sending out the same vibrational frequency as the manager or colleagues you are having problems with. In addition to that, you should analyze what bothers you about this person. Are you guilty by any chance of doing the very same thing with other people? At any rate, raising your vibrational frequency will put you into a totally different situation. If you are no longer on the same frequency as the other person and there is nothing more to be learned, the Universe will help you to improve this relationship or contrive for the two of you to go separate ways. You might in fact be transferred into another office or find a new job that you are more interested in, or your manager/colleague might decide to retire years earlier than expected, or your boss/colleague will suddenly start treating you very well. See page 51: "How can I raise my vibrational frequency?"

I like my job but I feel stressed out. What should I do?

Stress is the indication that you are not living in the moment. You – just as anyone else – can only do one thing well at a time. If somebody else is pushing you to do more things simultaneously, calmly ask your superior to prioritize your work, so you know which are the most urgent tasks to perform first of all. A person who is stressed out at work is unproductive for any company and releases vibrations that are bound to attract all sorts of other negative situations. So put your mind and heart in what you are doing and put aside all thoughts you have of the pile of things you need to get done, because thinking about the pile will just make you feel worse. Most of us always have a mountain of things to do but it's our attitude toward the pile that has to change – so let's focus solely on our Here-and-Now and let go of the rest.

I like my job but I am not earning as much as I would like to. What should I do?

If others are doing your same job and performing the same way as you are - or worse - but are getting lots more than you are, you are probably preventing yourself from accessing the flow of abundance. First evaluate whether you have been brought up with the idea that money is bad, as that concept can be stored in your subconscious and can be blocking the pay raise you want. A weak desire of earning more is also unproductive. Are you just complaining about not earning enough and doing nothing else about it? By focusing on the thought that you are not earning enough, you are just consolidating that reality. A strong desire is instead accompanied with a precise plan: I am going to earn (US$) by (date) and in order to achieve my goal I will do X, X and X. See the *Wish Come True Technique* on page 41 for the steps to take in the right direction.

Is it right to be ambitious or should we aim for the bare minimum?

We should endeavor to reach our full potential in our lifetime, which doesn't mean simply accumulating more and more. It means instead that we should learn and experience and enjoy... Once we have satisfied our basic needs of survival - air, water, food, shelter, clothing, education and good personal relationships – everything else is "extra".

Which are the most important personal qualities in any job?

Honest, enthusiastic, optimistic, patient, kind and respectful to others, well-organized and empathetic.

How can I attract the job I desire?

One way is to dress the part. By wearing the clothes that are socially accepted in the job role of your choice, it is much easier for you to attract the job you desire. The first reason is that if you dress for the job, you can begin to actually *feel* like the professional/employee/worker you want to be and start to attract it into your life experience. In addition, it is easier for others to imagine you suitable for the position offered if your appearance matches the job role in their minds. So if you want to work as a hardhat for a construction company, don't go looking for a job with a tie and dainty shoes; if you want to work in a lawyer's office, don't go to the interview with sagging pants that reveal your underwear; and don't you dare enter the door of a fashion designer dressed as the little match girl. You might be the world's greatest carpenter, paralegal or creative director but if you don't dress the part you will have a hard time getting past the first interview.

For the other steps involved in attracting the job you desire, see page 41 – the *Wish Come True Technique.*

I am looking for a job. What should I put in my resume?

Your resume should be concise, neat-looking and perfectly written, without any spelling or grammar mistakes. Unless otherwise indicated by the company seeking collaborators, if you are good looking you should by all means insert your photo. It should be a photo just of your head, somewhat like a passport photo but you should be smiling and look confident and helpful. Make sure you include information on your education, your qualifications, your previous work experience and your personal qualities. If you do not have previous work experiences to mention, specify why you are suitable for the position offered and which benefits your future employer would have by choosing you of all people. If you can't imagine why anyone would want to hire you of all people, why should they want to do so? To be able to find a job you have to believe in yourself, believe that you are a good choice, that you can truly be of value to a company. A resume should above all be *truthful*. Do not say that you perfectly know three foreign languages unless you really do. Do not invent talents that you do not have. If you are lacking in skills, then take the courses offered by the employment/unemployment office in your area or other organizations.

Once your resume is ready, send it to the right person. If you don't know the name of the right person, phone and ask for the name and email address of the Human Resource Manager or recruiter. Send out as many resumes as possible to companies so that you have more chances of being selected for an interview.

Most important of all, imagine in your mind what the Human Resource Manager will think when he/she is looking at your resume. Decide in advance that the Human Resource Manager will look carefully at your resume and choose yours to bring to the boss. Then go further in this mental creative process. The managing director looks at your resume and...

Besides describing my previous studies and work experience, what is important in a job interview?
You should also explain why you stand out with respect to other job applicants. What makes you more desirable for a company to have you as a collaborator? You should obviously think this out and know what to say before appearing at the job interview. You should also research the company and see if it produces or sells a product or service that is of value to others. Is it

a company that you would be enthusiastic about working in or would you do it half-heartedly? Is it fairly close to your residence or would you have to spend a lot of precious time getting to the company and back? You need to know these things before wasting your time and the recruiter's time.

Your body language is also decisive in a job interview, starting from the way you greet and shake hands with the interviewer/s. A person with a firm handshake is seen as having a strong personality, while a limp handshake indicates a lack of self-confidence. Everything – absolutely everything – of your exterior aspects are taken into consideration during a job interview, including your clothing. Not only should you dress the part, but your clothes should be neat and clean, your body should be clean, your teeth brushed, your hair washed and tended to. Be careful to keep your back straight - no slouching allowed - and do look your interviewer/s in the eyes. Also important is the tone of your voice. Does it sound respectful, enthusiastic and self-confident or hesitant, icy and distant? What is even more important is that before going to the job interview, you have visualized in your mind's eye exactly how you want the interview to go. Decide beforehand how you will be treated, that you will be chosen for the job and everything will go as you have planned.

I have a project in mind. When do I know if I should go ahead with it or not?

If you are uncertain about a project, if you don't really believe that it can be successful, then do not proceed. Your personal reality is based on your beliefs, thoughts and intentions, therefore your project would end up being unsuccessful if you went ahead and ignored your feelings. It's better to wait until you feel enthusiastic, certain, confident, believing...

I have an idea in mind but don't know what are the first practical steps to take. What should I do?
First of all make sure that you truly believe in your idea, that your idea would be of value to others and that you would enjoy doing the work that is involved.
The next step might not seem really practical at all to you but it actually is, as you are basically attracting your *finalized* idea into your life experience. It consists in focusing your attention daily on your idea. Dedicate about 15 minutes to this, preferably before going to sleep or upon awaking. Close your eyes and imagine that your idea has become a reality. This is not idle daydreaming but an essential step of the co-creation process. Every time you should imagine another scenario happening, but always revolving around your completed idea. The more you do this, the more you will receive intuitions to be acted upon and attract the final result into your life experience.

For example, if your idea is to invent a new means of transporting children, imagine receiving an email from a reporter asking how you got your brilliant idea in the first place and imagine yourself replying. Then see yourself taking a walk a few days later and passing by the newspaper stand, where you buy a magazine. You later decide to go to the park, you choose a bench in the warm sun, sit down and start leisurely reading the magazine. A

> *photograph of someone familiar strikes your attention, you sit up straight, you notice the man at the nearby ice cream stall looking at you oddly, oh my gosh is that really a picture of you in the magazine? You read the article and relish every word written about you and the fantastic invention that has noticeably improved the lives of children and their parents. You make a mental note of contacting that friend of yours who is an export expert. If your new product is so successful in the U.S., why shouldn't it be sold in Europe too? (...)*

I have an idea in mind but I'm not so sure that I'm the right person to carry it out. How can I boost my self-confidence?

If you are uncertain about your capabilities, it's practically impossible for you to successfully carry out your idea. Your doubts are in fact major obstacles preventing you from achieving success. To eliminate them and boost your self-confidence, stay away from people who belittle or limit you and envision yourself determined, powerful, resourceful, special... Because you can be any way you want to be and see yourself as being. If you've made the mistake in the past of underestimating yourself, now think of yourself as the best – or as in Tina Turner's song "Simply the Best".

I have started a new project but I have encountered obstacles. Is this a sign that I should drop the project?

It's a pity to drop your project after experiencing a few obstacles – it's like giving up early in the game. The primary reasons that new projects do not make it to the final stage is: drop of enthusiasm/interest and lack of perseverance. Obstacles and contrasts in themselves are not signs that you shouldn't proceed. They just mean that there is something that you have to deal with and resolve from a different viewpoint. Contrasts and obstacles force us to learn something new and grow. Therefore consider obstacles simply as temporary hurdles. When faced with an inconvenience, take time to think of a viable solution or readapt your initial plan to get your project into working order, for instance by engaging someone else's expertise or by using another type of material, or by moving the location to another place.

Most important of all is not to make the mistake of feeling emotionally overwhelmed. Don't give in to desperate thoughts such as: "My God, why have you abandoned me?" Be cool and keep your vibrational frequency high. Do the best you can and no more than that. All is well...

What are the most important personal qualities for a boss?

A tyrannical, glacial superior is counterproductive for a company. A good boss is a person who treats everyone with respect and helps his/her subordinates to learn and grow. He/she is honest, friendly, well-organized, a decision-maker, acts with the company's priorities in mind, possesses crisis management skills and is never lacking in self-control.

WEALTH & SOCIAL STANCE

Is money evil?

Money isn't evil, nor is it good. It's just a symbol that makes it easier for us to exchange goods and services. In our world, money is important as it provides us with more freedom to be, to do and to have what we want.

I am earning good money but how can I become rich?

If you desire to be rich, you first need to convince your mind that not only is it possible, not only is it *probable,* but it's *TRUE* that richness will become a part of your personal experience. Be generous with others – those who are stingy are preventing themselves from becoming rich and/or from enjoying what they have, because a stingy person believes "there is not enough", while richness means "there is plenty". Invest in yourself, by learning how to speak in public, discovering how to communicate better, finding out more about your business field. Also dress rich, which helps other people perceive you as full of money and you too will start changing the way you think about yourself. You will be in fact start *feeling* rich and it's this very feeling – and not working a double, stressful job – that will help you to attract economical abundance into your life experience. In addition, use your imagination to help attract richness, preferably before going to sleep or upon awaking.

For example, imagine yourself going to the bank, asking for your balance and seeing your account with six or more digits in the black. The bank manager notices you, comes up to say hello and hands you a beautiful aquamarine leather portfolio and engraved pen. You thank him while making a mental note of giving these to your chef, who is so talented in making you and your family heavenly meals. You then decide to take a walk downtown. It's Mother's Day next week and you start thinking about what your mom would like while you are walking by the shop windows. You have already made plans to pick her up for a fun excursion to Lake Garda but you'd also like to get her a little something to open on her special day. You know she doesn't care too much about diamonds but that she goes nuts for opals. You enter a jewelry shop, where you are shown a vast array of opals and you finally choose one that is green with flecks of blue, which reminds you of her eyes. You pull out your platinum credit card while the nice shop assistant gently places the pendant into a precious little box. You step out of the shop imagining your mother's face upon opening her present, which you will give to her on that beautiful terrace restaurant overlooking the lake. (...)

Is it wrong to want material things?

Everything existing in the physical world is made of energy and has its origin in the spiritual world. All material objects have been co-created by us through our thoughts and intentions. Desiring material things is natural and legitimate. A nice house to live in, without having to pay rent, is something that most of us desire. Having pretty clothes that look good on us, having a reliable car that is the pleasant to the eye and that gets us where we want to go are other natural, common desires.

Our ultimate goal however is not to have more money, more cars, more houses, more objects... Our highest objective is to live a life of joy and to bring joy to others. If we are focused on accumulating/collecting rather than enjoying what we have, we are then pretty far from our life's objective.

Is it difficult to become rich?

Don't think that it's difficult to become rich or that richness is reserved only for very intelligent or very hardworking people. Toiling is definitely *not* the way become rich, as it denotes hardship and stress. Fortunes are made by providing others with a wonderful product or service and by *feeling* rich.

Which conditions can prevent me from becoming rich?

If you feel poor, you can't attract richness. You can only become rich if you *feel* rich. If you believe that having lots of money is sinful, that too distances you from the pot of gold at the end of the rainbow. Negative emotions also prevent us from becoming rich, such as envy, greed, stress, anger...

How can I attract more money into my life?

See page 41 for the *Wish Come True Technique.*

What if I become rich by stealing or harming people in other ways?

Those who manage somehow to get a lot of money through stealing or harming people in other ways, such as selling brain-devastating drugs or other toxic products, can only attract misery into their lives. They may or may not feel guilt or remorse for what they do but they definitely cannot be happy, joyful people and will end up attracting negative events and circumstances in their personal reality. Of what use is money if the way you make it deprives you of joy and happiness?

Is poverty a virtuous condition?
Though some religions have instilled the notion that poverty is a virtuous condition and that being rich is shameful, there is no virtue in being poor nor is it virtuous to be rich. Not having enough though does connotate that something is wrong in your life. We are on planet Earth to thrive, enjoy and love and if this is not happening, we need to reassess our priorities, our thoughts, intentions, words and actions.

If I become rich do I deprive others in some way?
We live in a zero-limits Universe, where there is economical abundance for all who want it, so it's impossible for you to deprive others from having money or anything else.

It is true however that if you become rich by taking advantage of other people, for example by paying them salaries that do not allow them to live with dignity or by requiring them to work 9 or more hours a day, you *are* depriving others. Depriving others is a double-edged sword: you may momentarily receive economical abundance but you are preventing yourself from spiritually evolving and you are sure to attract negative events and circumstances into your life, since like attracts alike.

LOVE & RELATIONSHIPS

Which is the greatest sentiment in the human experience?
Love is definitely the greatest attribute of all, not only on planet Earth but in the entire Universe. Love is our link to the Creator.

Who am I in respect to others?
We are all one, as we all spring from the same source. The Flower of Life symbol clearly shows our interconnection. Each of our individual thoughts, words and deeds has repercussions on the others.

Of what value are relationships in my life?
How we relate to others is the most important aspect of our lives. Though we are individuals, each with a soul, distinctive thoughts and ambitions, no man is an island. The way we consider others, how we speak to others, the actions that we do – or don't do – to others are fundamental in shaping our personal reality. One of our challenges is to accept others for what they are – therefore to allow them the freedom of being who they want to be, even if we are not in agreement with their points of view. Though others can contribute to make us happy, our happiness shouldn't depend on any single person.

How can I learn to love others?
   A. First learn to love yourself
If you don't love yourself, how can you love others? Begin by opening your heart to yourself,

acknowledging your good qualities and your momentary weaknesses, and learn to be a satisfied and happy citizen of the world. Being an example of happiness is of benefit to anyone crossing your path.

B. Remember that everyone just wants to be loved
Just like you, everyone else wants to be respected and loved. Remember that your desires are basically the same as those of others.

C. Refrain from judging others
Though our opinions may differ from others, who are we to say that we possess the absolute truth? Respect others – what they think is the result of their personal experiences and current state of evolution. We can be totally in disagreement with their ideas but nonetheless respectful.

D. Never indulge in irate or aggressive behavior
If you're upset by someone else's behavior towards you, try to reply calmly, explaining your point of view. If you are not in control of your emotions, it's better to change the subject or turn away in silence rather than to react with anger. This is not always something easy to do but it is what distinguishes a mature, balanced person. It may take a lot of practice to master this, but you will be successful if you put your mind to it. Someone else's words and actions can anger you only if you let yourself be angered by them. Do not allow someone else to deprive you of your serenity. There is no reason you should remain in the presence of people who exhibit irate or aggressive behavior and there is no reason for you to indulge in such behavior either.

E. Try to understand what the others feel
By endeavoring to comprehend how someone is feeling, by imagining what the person is going

through, it is easier to relate to and love others. Empathy is a trait that opens your heart.

F.   Be happy for the success of others
Another feeling that opens your heart is rejoicing for your colleague's promotion, for your friend's gorgeous new house on the beach, or for your acquaintance's trip around the world.

G. Do unto others as you would have them do unto you
Never say words or do things to others that you would dislike for others to say or do to you. What is more, say words and do things to others that you know you would appreciate if you were in their shoes.

How can I demonstrate my love to someone?
A smile, a hug, a nice thought, kind words and helpful actions are all demonstrations of love.

Does everyone deserve to be loved?
We are all divine essences and each of us deserves to be loved. This does not mean that we have to put up with people who have decided to act aggressively. We can love them yet decide not to share our lives with those people.If you have a hard time loving them owing to their bad behavior, try to see them through the eyes of a loving mother.

What do I get out of being kind to someone?
If you are kind to others, you will be rewarded aplenty. Your kindness, your generosity, your respectful and thoughtful attitude towards others will allow you to attract equally delightful situations into your life experience.

Is altruism a virtue?
It's beautiful to contribute towards making someone happy, but you shouldn't forsake your own happiness for others. If you are always trying to please someone else, ignoring your own desires, you will see that what you do is never enough for them. You will have much better relationships if you are attentive to your emotions and do only what you feel good about doing.

How can I be of service to others?
Be alert and offer assistance when you see someone in need, whether it's helping your neighbor to throw out the trash, or carrying an elderly man's groceries to his car, or giving your seat on the bus to a pregnant woman, or inviting a lonely acquaintance over for a cup of tea and a chat. A lot of people don't *notice* others in need − train yourself to be present in the Here-and-Now and do not be shy.
Other ways to be of service to others is to donate money, goods or time to charitable organizations. Do not however donate money if you don't have much of it and do not offer your time if you are short on time...

Do I attract all the people who are in my reality?
Everyone who is a part of your reality has been invited into your life by you and no one else. You have attracted these people either because you are vibrating at the same frequency as they are (like attracts like) or because there is something that you need to learn from these relationships. Analyze the type of people that are currently a part of your life. What characteristics do they have? Are they kind and loving people or are they complaining and quarrelsome? If you have attracted

negative people, you can change the situation at any time by raising your vibrational frequency. By changing your negative thoughts, words and actions into positive ones, the people who surround you will gradually vanish from your life scene and more desirable people will begin to step in.

Should I abide by the saying "Live and let live"?

Each individual is the creator of his/her own life and attracts people, events and circumstances with matching vibrational frequencies. So it's really not up to you to make them change their different ways of being with respect to how you live your life. You can lovingly provide suggestions based on your own experience and you can be an example of virtue and joy but you should refrain from trying to oblige someone else to believe what you believe in or to act as you want them to act. We are all creators of our life experience with the gift of free will and no one on planet Earth has been appointed to force others to conform to his/her personal beliefs. What you can do is to teach them, if they are willing to listen to you, that there is an easier way to live life, that they can lead a much happier life if they would just notice their emotions and be daily conscious of the words they say and the actions they take.

What are the characteristics of the companion that we attract?

For two people to be able to attract each other as companions, they have to have matching vibrational frequencies – like being on the same radio frequency band. Couples are formed by two individuals who

116

complement each other, in the sense that each partner has one or more characteristics that the other partner doesn't have but would like to have. In most cases, we choose our life companion before reincarnating.

> *Back in 1992, I was working in the Italian office of a multinational company and a man had been hired as a show manager for a new trade show. He was a very reserved type of person and though we were in a small office, I had nothing to do with his job and he had nothing to do with mine, so there were no points of contact. I remember a colleague asking me: "What do you think of Marco?" I had replied vaguely about his being unfathomable and that I hadn't given him much thought. Everything changed for me after I had a dream not so long afterwards. I dreamt that he and I were under a big tree and felt overwhelming love for each other. That was all. We now have a son and have been together for 24 years. I am convinced that the spiritual world made our paths meet, though I cannot say whether Marco and I planned this together before reincarnating.*

I love someone who is married and will not leave his/her spouse. Should I settle for second best?
We have the gift of free will so we can do as we please. We can choose to belittle ourselves and demean ourselves and wait a lifetime for our lover to discover that we deserve to be number one in his/her heart. We can let our whole life go by, without forming our own family, because we keep on waiting for our lover to recognize us as Who We Really Are. If

you are attentive to your emotions and feel happy in your lover's presence nonetheless, all is well, but if you don't, well then it's time to change.

I love someone who doesn't love me. What should I do?

There is no magic potion to tie someone to you that doesn't want to be tied, and even if there were, how could you call this love? Love is to allow others to live as they want to live, to let them pursue their personal desires and ambitions. If you have tried to capture someone's interest but that someone simply isn't interested – or is no longer interested, let him/her go and turn your attention to others who are on your same vibrational frequency.

Why should I ignore or avoid negative people?

Negative people can be a part of your personal experience only if you have attracted them into your life or if there is something that you have to learn from your relationship with them. People who make you feel bad, who humiliate you, who constantly point out your weaknesses, who talk bad, do bad things or always leave you feeling sad or deprived of energy should be avoided as much as possible. Notice your feelings in the presence of people and if they are unpleasant sensations, then do not persist in spending time with them, as by continuing to do so, you will be influenced by their negative vibrations and risk attracting other negative people, events and circumstances into your life. Instead seek and preserve those relationships that leave you feeling good.

How should I react to people who are offensive or aggressive?

When provoked, never give way to emotional catastrophes, such as hitting, yelling or slamming a door. We should learn how to keep our cool when someone has been offensive or aggressive to us. Someone else's behavior shouldn't turn our usually-placid selves into brutes. We can't change how others are, but we can change the way we react to others. In our lifetime, we experience all sorts of contrasts, including people who lie, insult, ridicule or physically hurt us. Those people have lost touch with their divine origins and we shouldn't allow them to drag us down to their level.

Observe your negative emotion or thought objectively, neutrally, as if you were not involved. Open your heart. If you can't forgive, then ignore. Walking away, turning your mind from something unwanted to something wanted is always better than reacting violently.

Do irate and dishonest people get away with everything this way?

Irate and dishonest people will attract their own punishment, such as getting in touch with other irate and dishonest people or experiencing other unhappy events. Aggressive people shouldn't provoke a negative reaction in you but should kindle your compassion and love for them.

Is forgiveness a sign of weakness?

Forgiveness is a sign of great strength. It's a sign that you are not one to waste your energy in seeking revenge, but that you feel sorrow and compassion for the person who has hurt you.

What type of person is it preferable for me to hang out with?

Always ask yourself if the people you spend your time with give you good emotions. Do they make you smile, laugh, feel good about yourself? Or do they make you feel uncomfortable or diminished in any way? Do you hide your true thoughts and intentions from them because you are afraid you won't be understood? Choose good, positive people to hang out with, people who are in control of their emotions, who share their emotions and who treat you well. There is nothing written in stone that says you have to continue to see people who are noxious.

I want to be accepted. Should I give in to peer/social pressure?

When we do or say things that are not in line with Who We Really Are, we are faking an attitude that is not beneficial to anyone, starting from ourselves. By conforming to what others say and do, we are stripping ourselves of our magnificence. By abiding to someone else's desires, rather than our own, we are renouncing our divine nature. Giving in to peer or social pressure is always counterproductive, so be attentive to your emotions and make sure that you are not forsaking your values or desires to please anyone.

What are the ideal qualities in a companion?

Ideal companions might have elective affinities, starting from the same evolutionary level, but they also might not. Both parties might share, for example, a common spiritual objective and values such as honesty, kindness, integrity and empathy. The two parties may instead be very different one from another, with each party teaching and each party learning a life lesson. An ideal marriage is thought to be based on love and respect for each other's thoughts, ambitions and desires, but sometimes the imperfect companion we choose can help us to better learn and more quickly evolve than someone who would seem perfect to our eyes.

How can I attract an ideal companion into my life?

If you want to attract an honest, kind, empathetic and honorable companion into your life, you need to match the vibrational frequency of honesty, kindness, empathy and honor. Think well about the qualities that you deem essential in a relationship and then take the necessary steps to attract your soulmate (see page 41 for the *Wish Come True Technique*).

How can I keep my marriage happy?

A. Love yourself

To be able to get along with others, we must first love ourselves and be balanced.

B. Love, respect, honor and praise your spouse

We do not *have to* be in a relationship, nor do we *have to* get married. Marriage is something that we *choose* to do, that states our intention of sharing life together as a family, of growing and evolving together. Do not take your spouse's kindnesses for granted. Treat your spouse as a best friend, with love and respect. Give praise when praise is deserved.

C. Do not try to bend your spouse's will to your wishes

One of the problems of marriage is conflicting desires. One spouse wants to do one thing on Saturday afternoon and the other spouse wants to do something else. So who wins? Are the two destined to go their separate ways? That is sometimes the solution but it shouldn't always be like that as the couple would end up not sharing anything at all together... So the both of you ought to find balance, a little give and take.

D. Do not complain about your spouse to other people

By pointing out and discussing your spouse's faults with other people, you are focusing on negative thoughts and forcing the person you are speaking to have negative feelings as well. Talking to someone else about your spouse's behavior is only of benefit if you really want someone else's assistance and point of view, otherwise refrain from spreading negativity.

E. Be careful about your words and actions towards your spouse

We are usually less careful about our words and actions towards close family members, such as spouses, when it should actually be the opposite... Shouldn't we show our deepest love and consideration for our wife or husband - the single person we have chosen among all of Earth's inhabitants? By consciously choosing to be an example of balance and harmony, by doing acts of kindness, by heeding your emotions, by noticing your spouse's moods and helping him/her to get back into a serene state of mind, you will contribute towards making your marriage a happy one.

Is jealousy a sign of love?

Two people who decide that they are in a relationship together should respect their special bond, reassure each other of the exclusivity of their bond, and never do anything that betrays or offends the other. Jealousy just means that you are not sure that your partner is faithful or that you feel insecure about yourself. If you believe that your partner is unfaithful, obtain evidence before accusing him/her. If you are instead feeling insecure about yourself, then it's something you have to resolve within yourself. Do not limit your spouse's freedom by preventing him/her from meeting up with friends or going to painting/yoga/dance courses. If you're constantly afraid that your spouse is going to meet other attractive, interesting people that are better than yourself, you may run the risk of attracting that scenario into your life experience. You do not own your spouse. Your companion is a man or woman who is currently in a relationship with you but has the freedom at any time to break that relationship if you are no longer compatible. That doesn't mean that we should get into relationships and break up at our every whim. A healthy relationship means commitment and empathy.

Is divorce spiritually acceptable?

No one in the spiritual world will judge or condemn you if you decide to divorce your spouse. The decision of divorcing shouldn't however be taken lightly but be well thought through, especially if there are children involved. Do you want to break up your marriage because you have a crush for a new colleague or because your spouse mistreats you or your children?

Are you truly an unhappy couple? Do not take rash decisions but calmly reflect on the pros and cons of being together and try to imagine your new life without your spouse. If it's your spouse that wants to divorce you, endeavor to improve your behavior. But there is no way we can force someone to return our love, nor can we oblige a person to stay with us forever.

Should homosexuality be allowed?

We cannot limit the freedom of another person. We cannot prevent someone else from being, doing or having what he or she wants to be, have or do. We may not understand it and we may not want for homosexuality to be propagated, but it is not a sin, nor a virtue.

How can my emotions help me understand where I am with respect to the relationships in my life?

Our emotions always help us to realize the status of a relationship. How do we feel in the presence of the other person? If we feel ill at ease or any other negative emotion, that means that we are vibrationally discordant. This doesn't mean that the relationship will *never* be harmonic but only indicates the current incompatible state.

If We Are One, shouldn't I accept everyone into my life?

It's true that we all originate from one Source but having been given the gift of free will, we have individually chosen to have certain experiences and have evolved differently from each other. Our spirits and souls have thus gradually differentiated themselves from each other, based on our individual thoughts and intentions, words and actions. Each being is a complex result of a cumulation of aspirations, feelings, circumstances and events experienced from its divine origin to the current moment. Our Universe therefore features an enormous variety of different ways of being - differing points of view, different ways of reacting, different desires - and it's not always easy to understand each other. We can love our neighbor - in the sense that we recognize that our neighbor is a divine essence like us and though he/she may currently be less-spiritually evolved than us, he/she does have our same basic aspirations. We can love without necessarily having to agree or put up with our neighbor's behavior.

We also have to remember that we are on planet Earth to experience contrasts, learn from these and evolve, so each time we are confronted with a situation in which someone does something that bothers or hurts us, we should first look ourselves in the mirror to see if we too are guilty of having that same behavior towards other people. If we discover that we too are at fault, we can correct our ways and we will find that others will no longer have that behavior towards us.

If We Are One, shouldn't everyone accept me into their lives?

We are in harmony only with whom we are vibrationally compatible to. Our lifelong goal should be to love others - whether we are vibrationally compatible or not, whether we agree with what they say and do or not - while staying true to Who We Really Are. Others may or may not accept us and love us in return, but the important thing is that our hearts are open.

How can we improve our relationship with people we cannot move away from, such as family members?

A. Self-analysis

Always attempt to understand why others are interacting with you in the worst of ways. Is it really just our relative's fault? Did your tone of voice or something you said spark their negative reaction? It might be that you are inadvertently doing something that is irritating to others. Self-analysis is therefore the first step to take.

B. Learn how to react to contrasts in a better way

Sometimes we need to change the way we are reacting to people – to be less touchy, to be more in control of our emotions, to be more aware and more understanding of the other person's current state of evolution.

C. Raise your vibrational frequency and things will change

When we raise our vibrational frequency – by opening our heart, saying kind words, doing things that make us joyful – we dramatically improve our relationship with others, including family members with whom we previously had a rough time.

If a family member has however truly behaved in an outrageous way towards us, there is no spiritual law that says that we are forced to continue in this relative's presence. Forgiving and walking away is a viable option.

But what if we can't walk away for some reason? In that case, instead of dwelling over what he/she said or did, open your heart, and state aloud that you and the other person <u>will</u> find a way to get along well, no matter what. And what if we don't want to forgive? The problem is that the Universe will keep placing this relative in our path until we find a way to pardon and move on with our life...

How can I reconnect with someone who is important for me?

If you are interested in reconnecting to this person, try to understand what is going on in his/her head and life. Then take the first step. Don't wait for the other person to approach you, even though you might feel that he/she should be the first...

I feel hurt by something that someone has said or done to me. What should I do?

Too many times we do not tell those you have hurt us that we feel offended. We pretend that all is okay but we grieve in our heart. Communicate your feelings to the person and you might be surprised to know that it was never his intent to treat you badly.

If the person has intentionally harmed you, forgive him nonetheless. He has only done what it is plausible for him to do at his current state of evolution. By opening your heart, forgiving and giving the person another chance you will feel so much better.

How powerful are the words I say?

Though words in themselves are not powerful, if they are uttered with emotion, they can hold immense power – either in a helpful or a in harmful way. Be very careful about the words you say, as your emotion-filled words attract people, circumstances and events into your life that you may not desire. If you talk about sickness, you will attract disease. If you talk about it being impossible to find a job, you will never find a job. If you talk about the neighborhood being plagued by thieves, your house will be robbed. If you talk about being poor, you will continue to be poor or even poorer than before...

So prior to talking, reflect. Before communicating verbally, think whether you are about to speak about something that is unpleasant and undesirable. If that is so, it is in your interest to refrain from speaking at all. On the other hand, by all means talk about what is pleasant and desirable. We attract what we think about because of the Law of Focused Thought Manifestation (see page 26 – point C: "What are the laws that rule our Universe?").

How can I deliberately improve my relationships with others?

We can remarkably enhance our relationships with others just by smiling, which is a way of opening our heart. Always be aware of the fact that the person in front of you may not on your same footing, so to speak. The person may be having a lousy day and may not be in control of his/her words and acts, as you have learned to be. Strive to be an example of balance and harmony. Do not let anyone else's negativity drag you down to their level and be faithful to your true essence.

Someone dear has distanced himself/herself from me although I have been aligned with who-I-really-am. Why has this happened?

In our lifetime, we meet and remain in contact (either willingly or unwillingly) only with:

- people with whom we are vibrationally harmonious - that is, with people who are on our same vibrational frequency. If we are no longer vibrationally similar, each of us will attract people who are on their same vibrational "channel";

- people from whom we need to learn something. Once we learn that something, the person will vanish from our scenario.

I now understand the Laws of the Universe and want to teach others about them. How can I convince them that they are true?

If you have spiritually awakened, that doesn't mean that others are ready to awaken. Remember how unbelieving you were prior to awakening... People are not always receptive to believing in concepts that the masses haven't accepted as truth. So you can talk about the Laws of the Universe to others and try to explain to them how much good it has done you to know about the Laws. You can mention the Law of Vibrational Attraction and the Law of Focused Thought Manifestation and point out the changes that have occurred to you thanks to these Laws, but you cannot convince anyone. In addition, no one *should* believe in anything just because someone else says that it's true. Blind faith and blindly accepting dogmas is pure ignorance. We are divine beings who are meant to use our own minds and not passively accept somebody else's ideas.

If you have awakened, you truly desire to share the path to love and happiness with others who are close to you. When you see the mistakes they make - the same mistakes that you previously used to make, such as speaking negative, unkind words or exhibiting irate or aggressive behavior - you deeply desire to help them to discover the beauty of what you have learned. Do plant the seeds - do tells others what you have learned and be a living example of balance, harmony, virtue and joy - but do no more than that, because the rest is up to them.

PART 2
ABOUT DEATH

What is death?
Death does not exist - or rather, our physical body dies but our spirit continues to live forever. Death is therefore a grand illusion as it doesn't mark the *end* of our existence but a change of our consciousness to a higher vibrational level. Our pure essence - our spirit along with our soul - continues to exist and thrive in the non-physical plane of existence.

What happens when you die?
When we die, we usually go through the steps indicated here below, though not necessarily in this same order:

A. *Sense of serenity*
At the time of death, you no longer feel pain or other negative physical sensations, but you feel a sense of well-being, of peacefulness.

B. *Change of vibrational frequency*
Upon dying, you change vibrationally frequency, going from the denser realms of the physical world, to the higher vibrations of the spiritual world.
When your astral body is on the verge of freeing itself from your physical body, you may hear unusual sounds like a roar, rumble, thump or buzz, which indicate you are changing your vibrational frequency.

C. *Your astral body is freed from your physical body along with your consciousness*
The same body that you use when you sleep and that some consciously use for astral travel - your astral body - drifts away from your dead physical body along with your spirit and soul. When this happens, you may feel a floating, sliding, spinning or plunging/sinking sensation. The vibrations, sounds and other physical

133

phenomena you might have experienced earlier cease to be.

Your astral body resembles the physical body you had when alive but the living will not - in most cases - be able to see this spiritual body of yours. And in most cases, you will not be able to interact with the physical world, such as moving an object or speaking and being heard.

    D. You either realize that you are dead or you don't...

The majority of people who die realize that they are dead and that they have passed from one dimension (the physical plane) to another dimension (the spiritual plane), but this is not always the case...

        1. You don't realize that you're physically dead or you refuse to believe in anything besides the physical plane

        Some individuals totally ignore - in the sense that they do not realize - that they are dead as they can still see what appears to them to be the physical world. What they are instead seeing are the astral duplicates – or counterparts – of the physical world. Others instead realize that they are no longer alive physically speaking but are confused as to their new environment. Others yet think that they're having an extraordinarily long dream or refuse categorically to accept the fact that they are dead because they are so attached to the people or other circumstances in the material world. Some cannot fathom the thought that there is something else beyond physical, while others believe they have some unfinished business to tend to before abandoning the physical world.

These spirits therefore remain trapped, of their own accord, in the lower astral world that appears so much like the physical world, and we usually refer to them as ghosts or poltergeists. They continue to hang around where they lived when in-body and can sometimes be seen by the living.

Astral travelers or spiritually-elevated healers can help these confused or reluctant souls to proceed on their spiritual journey and gently persuade them to go towards the light.

2. *You realize that you're physically dead (most cases)*

Most individuals who die realize that they are no longer a part of the physical world yet understand that they are still very much alive.

IF YOU REALIZE THAT YOU ARE PHYSICALLY DEAD, YOU PROCEED ONWARDS:

E. You are free to explore the astral plane

You find yourself freed from the constraints and limitations of your physical body and feel an overwhelming sense of freedom.

Your astral body is no longer hindered by the physical laws, such as gravity, and it is much more thought-responsive compared to your physical body. So by thinking of a certain place, you can immediately be in that place. You are free to move about and explore the astral plane any way you like. You can run, walk, climb, jump, fly... You are no longer physical but you continue to be thought and emotion.

F. You may attempt to express your goodbyes to the living

Upon dying, many decide to stay close to the physical world for a few days and to express their goodbyes to their loved ones. Not everyone in the physical world is able to perceive this communication as it depends on our vibrational frequency, our sensitivity and the sentiment that connects us to the departed person.

G. You may be greeted by angels, guides, dead and alive friends or relatives

A welcoming party made up of dead friends and relatives, even from previous lives, as well as angels and spirit guides, will joyfully greet you and help you to proceed on your spiritual journey. Only those with whom you are in harmony with will be there. There may also be people who are still physically alive, who have used their astral bodies to be there, though they may not remember upon waking about having participated at this event.

H. You enter a tunnel or other passageway and go towards the light

Your guides will help you to enter a tunnel or other passageway. You will feel deeply compelled to go towards the brilliant light at the end of the tunnel, similar to the effect of a magnet. When you reach the light, you will feel embraced by pure love and positive energy, and it will feel to you as if you have returned to your real home.

I. You reunite with the spiritual energy you had left behind

When we reincarnate, we leave a part of our energy in the spiritual world, with which we reunite at the end of our physical life.

J. You meet with highly evolved spirits who help you to review your life

At this point, you will meet up with your spirit guide, the Council of Elders and/or a being of light, who will assist you in reviewing your entire life. You will see every detail of your life played back to you, as if it were a film. You will be able to examine it both objectively and subjectively, so you will relive your emotions and also feel the emotions that you caused in others by your words and actions.

Your guides will help you to reflect on what you have learned in that incarnation - also from the circumstances or events you pre-established before incarnating (Life Project) - and to pinpoint what you still need to learn. You are not judged by others – only you are the judge of the events of your life.

K. You reunite with your group of souls

Soul groups are spirits that choose to spiritually evolve together. The reported number of souls per group goes from a minimum of five to a maximum of 100. Our close family members - our parents, our brothers and sisters, and our children - are usually in our soul group. Some friends, acquaintances and colleagues that we know in our current physical lifetime may also be in our soul group. The members of the group share the same spiritual objectives and interact with each other both in the physical and in the non-physical worlds.

When we die we reunite with our soul group and plan our future challenges, deciding whether to return to the physical world again and with which other souls. The roles of souls vary from one physical life to another, therefore the soul that was your mother in one physical lifetime may be your daughter in another physical lifetime.

> *L. You remain in the astral world until you reincarnate in the physical world or you ascend to the higher plane of existence that is your vibrational match*

Depending on how we lived our last physical life, we go to the spiritual plane that corresponds to our energetic vibration. The highest spiritual level is the closest to the Creator, while in the lowest there is lack of light and love.

What if your dead relatives and friends have reincarnated in the meantime? Does that mean that you can't meet them when you die?

Even though your dear dead loved ones may have reincarnated, you can meet up with them nevertheless. Even if they are now in the physical world, they - as everyone else – can use their astral body during sleep to explore the spiritual world. In addition, when we incarnate, we leave a part of our spiritual energy in the spiritual world.

Is death different for those who practice certain religions?

The religious beliefs we hold on planet Earth do not intrinsically alter the way we experience death and our transition of consciousness. The afterworld will be no different for you whether you are a Christian, a Jew or an atheist.

However, when we die we initially go to the astral plane of existence, which is much more thought responsive than the physical world. In this plane, your thoughts, beliefs and expectations shape your environment much faster than in the physical world. For this reason, Christians may see Jesus or the Madonna, Muslims may see Muhammad or the 72 virgins and if you believe there is a hell with devils and fire and that you deserve to go there, that's what you'll experience. But once you realize how your thoughts and beliefs shape your environment, then you will be free to create your surroundings.

Rather than our religious beliefs, what does have a major impact on our new state of being is the way we each lived our life prior to death. Our spirit will continue to live in the non-physical plane of existence as it was when we were in the physical world. Dying does not secure instant enlightenment.

What happens to the people who have done evil things in their lives?

When they physically die, those who have caused suffering to others, as well as those who have committed suicide, do not proceed as the other spirits do towards the light. These souls feel such regret and guilt for their acts that they find themselves unworthy of coming close to the Creator. They are isolated from the others and undergo a purification process, which is not perceived to be a punishment but a method that helps spirits to rehabilitate their damaged souls. This does not mean that those who have done evil things in their lives get away with everything. They are made to understand the grief they have caused and they suffer from the acts they have done. Before they reincarnate again, they will decide in advance to experience certain situations (Life Project) which will help them to fully realize the impact of the words and acts on someone's life – in this case their own.

What happens to someone who has experienced a sudden death?

When someone dies during a sudden, traumatic event, such as in a fire, a car/train/plane accident, or drowning, the spirit usually separates itself from the body prior to physical death so that the person will no longer feel any physical pain. In some cases though the spirit remains within the physical body as there is something further that the soul needs to learn from having this experience.

Once the spirit and soul have separated from the physical body, the next step depends on whether the person realizes that he/she is dead or not and whether he/she accepts this fact. For obvious reasons, those who have experienced a sudden death usually find it harder to accept the fact that they are physically dead. (See page 134: "You either realize that you are dead or you don't...").

Do we choose when we die?

We do. It's our spiritual essence - our soul - that decides when it's time to leave the physical plane of existence and return to the spiritual world.

Our physical life comes to an end when:

A. We are no longer making progress with the life lessons we set out to learn. That is, we are feeling deeply unhappy without reacting, so that we consistently perceive our days to be grey, miserable or dull.

OR

B. We have learned everything that we set out to learn in this lifetime (though some decide to remain on to help others to evolve spiritually).

140

Do we choose how we die?

There is a meaning for *everything* in our life, including our death. The way we physically die holds purpose, either for ourselves or for the other people involved. There is therefore a lesson to be learned, an experience to be had, by us and/or perhaps by others. If we for example die a slow death, it may be that the people who find themselves at our bedside - who could be a caregiver, a family member, a doctor or a friend... - learn what it's like to give unconditional love and assistance. There is also a reason why we die in so-called accidents. Accidents are in fact never accidental, as they are either events you planned before coming into this physical plane of existence (your Life Project) or an event that you have attracted through your thoughts, words or deeds or through your focused attention to someone or something.

Why do some people die young?

Young people - even very young individuals, such as babies and fetuses - are no different from anyone else and die because:

- they have already learned what they set out to learn in this physical existence;

- they pre-planned to die young as a learning, spiritually-evolving experience for themselves or for someone else (Life Project);

- they do not react well to the environment they find themselves in and decide to just let go, abandon the physical world and return to the spiritual world;

- they have attracted an accident or serious illness that has led to their death, either through the Law of Vibrational Attraction or the Law of Focused Thought Manifestation (see page 26 – point C "What are the laws that rule our Universe?").

What happens during an abortion?

Giving birth is a beautiful gift that we give to another spirit, so that it has the opportunity of incarnating in and experiencing the physical world. Abortion is against nature, as it interrupts the life-giving process that is already underway, but the souls within fetuses are in some ways no different from any other souls. Though fetuses do not actively co-create their personal reality with their words or actions, they do co-create through their focused attention to someone or something (they sense how their mother feels and other sensations from the environment), and they too may have pre-established in their Life Project to experience certain events, which may also include the abortion itself.

Though the physical fetus dies, the spirit and soul of the unborn fetus never dies.

What hinders us from having a serene death?

Guilt from the behavior we have had during life. Do not wait until your last breath to pardon, love, and be free of negative emotions such as envy and grudges. Since our conscious minds are unaware of when our last day of life will be on planet Earth, let's do our best to speak words of kindness to everyone who we happen to encounter - whether they address us the same way or not – and to do acts of kindness to everyone crossing our path, as we would want for others to do to us. A serene death is knowing that you have really done your best.

What is the ideal spiritual preparation to make the transition to death?

One prerequisite is to let go of all your negative feelings, from resentfulness, to distrust, to blaming others for the things that have happened to you in your lifetime. We have to learn to accept that everything in our life has occurred for a reason, a purpose. *Everything.*

In addition, mindfulness is an important factor - that is, realizing that we are much more than our physical bodies, that we are indeed divine essences that are ready - or will be ready when the time is right - to go back to our true home where we will continue to exist. Those who are too tied to the material world and/or do not believe that anything besides the physical world exists risk becoming trapped between the physical and the astral planes when they die. These souls prevent themselves from ascending to the higher spiritual planes.

To develop a higher awareness of your spiritual nature, see page 236: "Which techniques can help me to grow spiritually?"

How can I help spiritually guide someone in making the transition to death?

If you believe that your presence is considered welcome and beneficial to the person who is about to make his/her transition to the afterworld, by all means stay by this person's side. Ask the Universe to assist you in this delicate moment and to help you to say words that are meaningful. Whether you believe that the dying person is capable of hearing you or not, soothe him and explain that all is well, that he will continue to live in another dimension where there is no longer pain. Avoid signs of bereavement and instead open your heart – allow the person to return peacefully to the spiritual world. Gently invite him to let go of repressed or expressed anger, guilt or other undesirable feelings. Explain that he is about to enter a wonderful world that is overflowing with love, a place where he can return to express his true, unique spiritual essence. Tell him to follow the light and to remember that in the afterworld he can manifest his desires much more quickly than on planet Earth, so that he will have much greater freedom. Let the person know that he will be accompanied to the light by his spirit guide and will be dearly greeted by his loved ones. Help the person savor and appreciate this very special moment, speaking when speaking is needed and remaining in silence, though present, otherwise.

Is burial or cremation preferable?

This is a very personal decision that is up to the dying individual, though it's true that with burial those who are less spiritually evolved might attempt to hang on to the physical world and close to their body rather than proceeding forward towards the light.

On the other hand, cremation may be viewed as traumatic for the less spiritually evolved and also for those who have died suddenly, which is why you shouldn't cremate someone immediately after death.

How long should you wait before cremating a dead person?
Wait at least three days after death, so that the person has the time to gain awareness of his/her new spiritual state before the physical body has been reduced to ashes.

How is suicide viewed in the spiritual world?
Suicide is a way of running away from your problems, but you can never really run away from your problems because you never really die... It's just your physical body that dies. So those who commit suicide soon discover that their problems don't vanish when they are physically dead. They realize how much suffering they've caused to themselves and to others, feel tremendous remorse and find themselves again in square one of the game... Suicide is considered one of the worst things a soul can do. Even though no one will judge them, they soon realize that they have broken the pact – their Life Project. They have dropped out of the Game of Life and wasted a chance to evolve.

When they physically die, those who have committed suicide do not proceed as the other spirits do towards the light. If they do not remain trapped between the physical and the astral worlds, they are isolated and undergo a purification process. This is not perceived to be a punishment but is instead a method that helps spirits to rehabilitate their damaged souls.

Could suicide have been included in one's Life Project before reincarnating?
No, suicide is not a condition that we could have inserted into our Life Project, so if we kill ourselves

we are violating our original intentions and ruining the chances we have at evolving spiritually. We are wasting the precious life lessons that we had set out to learn from.

Do our departed loved ones need prayers?

It depends on the spiritual evolution of our departed loved ones. We can pray for them - not by reciting a series of words that you have memorized - but by talking to them heart to heart. We can tell them that we are sad that they are no longer with us but that we will meet up with them again when our time comes. We can tell them that we forgive them and that we hope they will forgive us for our failings. We can tell them we have loved them and always will, and we can help them to move away from the physical world and go towards the light, where they will reunite with their true spiritual essence.

Should we mourn our departed loved one for a long time?

The dead shouldn't be detained in the physical world by those who are physically alive. Our long, drawn-out mourning may in fact prevent those who are dead to proceed on their spiritual path, keeping them in the lower astral planes. Our sorrow and pain sadden our dead loved ones, who want for us to get on with our life and attract wonderful events and circumstances that cannot reach us if we are in despair.

How can I get in touch with a loved departed one?

Our dead beloved may not be ready or willing to communicate with us, so do not force the situation.

146

Here are some ways we can attempt to get in touch with them:

A. Transmit your message through your focused thought and it will be received.

B. Out-of-body experience (OBE). Before attempting a self-induced OBE, focus your attention on your loved departed one, asking the person if he/she wants to meet up with you. In most cases, we get in touch with our loved ones through what we perceive to be as dreams, but these are actually out-of-body experiences, even if we are not conscious that they are so.

C. Automatic writing. Hold a pencil and place the tip of the pencil on a sheet of paper, without resting your wrist or any other part of your arm. Ask the person if he/she wants to communicate with you and let your hand be guided. At first the message may be incomprehensible or it may look like a doodle. Repeat regularly though not for more than 20-30 minutes per day. If you try this method, be aware that your mind may influence what you write.

D. With the help of a medium or a sensitive. Mediums and sensitives acts as a channel between the physical and spiritual world, transmitting communications from spirits to physical living beings and vice versa. The difference between a medium and a sensitive is that mediums allow for spirits to take over their body for the purpose of communication, while sensitives receive information from the spiritual world through their six senses. Make sure you engage the services of a professional, spiritually-evolved medium or sensitive.

The use of a ouija board is instead not recommended as a way to contact your dead loved one, since anyone in the astral world - even spirits who pretend they're your dear beloved - can appear and endeavor to play with your mind...

Do people who die have regrets?

Unfortunately, when we reach the end of our physical lives, many of us feel that we haven't accomplished all that we had originally planned to do. In most cases, we believe we have wasted a lot of precious time, that we have paid too much attention to unwanted things, that we haven't done much for others, and that we haven't lived the life of joy that we desired before coming into the physical world. This should act as a wake-up call for us who are still physically in-body, as we have the power to mend our ways and lead a successful, regret-free life.

Are we judged when we die?

No one will accuse or judge us at death. The only strict judge of our past physical life will be ourselves. We will be made to see that everything that we have done and everything we have gone through has been a learning experience for us.

Do we go to heaven or hell when we die?

No, heaven and hell do not exist. We all initially go to the astral plane of existence, whatever our conduct has been in the physical world. The astral plane is much more thought responsive compared to the physical world, so if you are convinced there is a hell and that you deserve to go there, you will then experience your own private hell. But once you realize - on your own or with the help of other spirits - that it's your thoughts, beliefs and expectations that shape your environment in the astral world, then you will be free to create your surroundings. Some souls however stay in the astral plane for a short period and proceed on to the other higher spiritual planes depending on their vibrational frequency. See page 156: "Which are the planes of existence?"

Do we become enlightened when we die?
No, when we leave the physical world, we keep everything of who we are, with the exception of our physical body. If we weren't wise, highly spiritually evolved and full of virtues before, we do not become instantly so when we die. We remain pretty much as we were before, with our same qualities and our same imperfections. Most of us though - those who realize that they are physically dead (see page 134 point D – "What happens when you die?") - do have a much wider and clearer vision of universal reality when we die, since we rediscover our soul's path, meet the Council of Elders, and reunite with our soul group. When we realize that the vibrational plane in which we find ourselves becomes limited for us, then we search for more and aim to progress to the next plane of existence.

What is a near-death experience (NDE)?
A near-death experience is a phenomenon observed by some people who have had bad accidents or very serious illnesses. Their physical body functions no longer work, so they are pronounced clinically dead,

but they experience being in another dimension and then return to physical life.

Which phenomena are observed during near-death experiences (NDE)?

Those who have had a near-death experience say that it's a powerful life-changing event. They have reported one or more of the following phenomena:

- sudden cessation of pain, replaced by a pleasant feeling;
- separation of astral body from their physical body;
- being able to see and hear what is going on near their physical body without however being able to communicate with anyone;
- going through a dark tunnel and coming into contact with spiritual guides or angels;
- detailed analysis or re-run of every person encountered and every action performed in their life;
- return to the physical body.

My childhood friend Sandro had a ski accident when he was a young man. He told me:
I remember that I saw my entire life in an instant, like an accelerated film... It was probably the adrenaline of that moment that pushed my neuronal activity to the max...however yes, I saw it all (or at least what I believe was all) in an instant.

PART 3
ABOUT THE
AFTERWORLD

LIFE AFTER PHYSICAL DEATH

What proof is there that life after death exists?

- *Out-of-body experiences (OBE)*
  See pages 218-234 "USING YOUR ASTRAL BODY WHEN PHYSICALLY ALIVE - OUT-OF-BODY EXPERIENCES (OBE)"

- *Past-life regression hypnosis*
  See page 182: "How can I find out about my previous life/lives?

- *Communications from our dead loved ones or other spiritual beings*
  See page 163: "How do spirits communicate with the living?"

- *Testimonies from people who have died and returned to life, also called Near Death Experiences (NDE)*
  See page 149: "What is a near-death experience (NDE)?"

- *Testimonies from spirits or groups of spirits*
  There are mediums who channel highly evolved spirits that wish to share their knowledge with all those interested in listening. Examples are: Esther Hicks, who channels a group of non-physical entities called Abraham; J.Z. Knight who channels Ramtha; and the late Jane Roberts who channeled Seth.

What does the afterworld look like?

The afterworld doesn't appear objectively but only subjectively. It in fact doesn't look the same for everyone. How you perceive the afterworld to be depends on your state of consciousness, on your thoughts, beliefs and expectations. You can actually shape your new environment howsoever you like. Some souls though feel reassured by re-creating the same surroundings which they were used to have in the physical world. Others may have pre-established ideas of what heaven, hell or limbo *should* look like and believe they *deserve* to be in heaven, hell or limbo, so they design their settings based on their beliefs and expectations. While we are all free to use our imaginations and paint our own afterworld using our favorite colors and inserting what pleases us the most, not all of us do so.

Are there churches, temples, etc. in the afterworld?
If you want or believe that there should be churches, temples or mosques in the afterworld, then there will be. When we evolve spiritually, we realize however that these structures are not necessary as all we need to connect with the Creator is an open heart.

Where is the afterworld located?
The afterworld is not in the sky above the Earth, nor below us, under ground – it is everywhere. This is another plane of existence that vibrates at a higher vibrational frequency than the physical world, so it cannot be seen by those who are physically alive.

What do spirits do in the afterworld?
Though spirits are free to do what they please, whatever they imagine is possible and pleasing for them to do, some self-limit themselves and continue to do what they used to do when physically alive, such as eat, sleep, go to work, go to the movies... Evolved

154

spirits have zero limits and consciously use their focused thought to create and do whatever they desire.

> *Many years after my friend Valeria had died young from cancer, I dreamt of her, though I now believe I actually saw her in the astral world. She was sitting on the floor with other people and was playing cards. This was something that she enjoyed doing when she was alive. I came near her to say hello. She turned around, looked at me but she didn't recognize me.*

Do spirits hang out with the same partners, relatives and friends in the afterworld as they did when physically alive?
This is a very personal choice. After death, you may meet again and continue to associate with - if you mutually wish to do that - with your close friends and relatives.

Do spirits continue to use the 5 senses as they did when physically alive?
Spirits do not have eyes to see, ears to hear with, nor any other physical senses but they may initially think they do as they are re-creating with their beliefs and expectations their environment. When they become aware that they no longer need to comply with the physical laws, spirits become more and more creative and free to truly express themselves.

What do spirits look like in the afterworld?
When you die, you initially pass from the physical world to the astral plane of existence. In this plane, your astral body is much more thought-responsive

compared with the physical world. Therefore, you appear the way your mind remembers yourself prior to dying or how you *desire* to appear. Your astral body thus may look exactly like your physical body at the time of death, or it may appear younger and prettier because you prefer to think about yourself and see yourself that way.

If and when spirits evolve, passing from the astral plane to the higher spiritual planes of existence, they may or may not preserve the same image. They might for example appear as globes of light, either white or other colors.

Which are the planes of existence?

There are said to be seven planes of existence, each of which has seven sublevels. They are called in many different ways depending on the various philosophies. The planes are listed here below from the lowest vibrational frequency to the highest:

1. *First plane of existence (Physical and Etheric planes)*

This is where we currently live. It is the densest and the slowest thought-responsive of the seven planes. We use our physical body in this plane.

The three lowest subplanes of the physical dimension are made up of material, liquid and gaseous substances, while the four higher subplanes are called etheric or double etheric as they are a perfect copy of the physical body.

2. *Second plane of existence (Astral or Emotional plane)*

This is where our astral bodies go when we dream and this is where our spirits first go when we physically die. There is no space nor time limit in the astral plane. The astral dimension is also different from the physical world as it's more thought-responsive and vibrates at a higher frequency than the material world. Spirits instantly create their own personal reality here based on their thoughts, beliefs and expectations, whereas in the physical world this process takes place much more slowly. In this dimension, spirits do not need to eat, drink, breathe or sleep but they might continue to do so because they want to or believe that they need to. Since the astral plane is less dense than the physical plane, the objects created by spirits in this plane using their minds are also less dense. The colors in this dimension are much more intense compared to the physical world.

Those who were very material-minded when physically alive remain in the astral world for a long time and sometimes indefinitely, so that they can fulfill all their desires using their mind. In this plane, damaged souls undergo a purification process. More spiritually-minded souls instead stay in the astral plane for a short time. The astral body dissolves when the soul is ready to pass over to a plane with a higher frequency.

3. *Third plane of existence (Causal plane/Mental plane)*

After leaving the astral world, spirits either enter the mental plane or reincarnate once again in the physical dimension. The mental plane vibrates at a higher frequency than the astral plane. This is where more highly evolved spirits, with a greater understanding that We-Are-One, express themselves by using their thoughts to visualize circumstances and events. Spirits use their mental body to interact in the mental plane of existence.

4. *Fourth plane of existence (Akashic plane/Intuitional plane/Buddhic plane)*

In this dimension, we find spiritually-evolved souls who are no longer ego-driven. Many of these souls are masters who desire helping others understand that We-Are-One. They interact in this dimension using their akashic body, which is the result of all of their soul's past lives. Spirits residing in this plane often go to the lower vibrating planes in order to communicate their wisdom to those living there.

5. *Fifth plane of existence (Spiritual plane/Atmic plane)*

Abstract intellectual energy, truth. This is the plane where we find angels and spirit guides.

6. *Sixth plane of existence (Messianic plane/Monadic plane/Anupadaka plane)*

Abstract emotional energy, love.

7. *Seventh plane of existence (Buddhaic plane/Divine plane/Adi/Logos)*

Pure energy. The soul becomes One with the Creator. Total enlightenment.

What is the Creator's energy like?

The Creator is the pulsating core of the Universe, somewhat like a beating heart.

The night after my second hatha yoga lesson, in October 2017, I "saw" what I instantly understood to be the Creator's energy. It was a very different experience from anything I had ever heard of or imagined. It appeared to me like an astonishingly powerful energy nucleus in expansion, surrounded by separate bands of energy. I

> *tried to get closer to the bands around the supreme force in the center and saw what looked at first glance as stars, but a closer look revealed that each band or layer had bright specks of light moving at different vibrational frequencies. It seemed to me that the fastest moving specks of light were the closest to the core. I felt awe and marvel at the same time.*

Are spirits free to go from one plane of existence to another as they please?

No. Spirits stay in the plane of existence that is in harmony with their own vibrational frequency. They can however pass over to other planes with lower vibrational frequencies in order to assist others who are in those other dimensions.

Who can you find in the astral plane?

See page 227: "Who can I meet during out-of-body experiences (OBEs)?"

How does one communicate in the astral plane?

The form of communication used in the astral world is telepathy. Thoughts and sensations are transmitted from one soul to the other soul via the mind and heart.

Do we keep our personality in the afterworld?

When we die, we keep our personality traits, such as our humor, our moodiness, our cheerfulness... We also preserve all our memories and everything we have learned from all our previous lives.

Do we continue to have emotions in the afterworld?

Definitely so. Emotions are the true indicators of Who We Really Are. We are divine sparks created from the greatest, most extraordinary emotion of all, which is Love.

When I am dead can I see my live loved ones?

Though you will no longer have physical eyes with which to see nor any other physical sense, when you are dead you will nonetheless be able to perceive how your live loved ones are feeling and what they are doing. If the physical living are sensitive and mindful enough, they will be able to receive the messages that you wish to communicate to them. Communication between the astral and the physical world is easier however during special moments of the in-body person's day: right before he/she falls asleep and immediately upon awaking (half-sleep).

What are ghosts?

Ghosts are spirits that were once like us, with a physical body. They either do not realize that they are dead or refuse to accept the fact that they are dead. This may be because they are so attached to their physically-alive loved ones or to their dwellings. Some spirits refuse to abandon the material world since their lives were fully committed to physical pleasures. Others yet feel that they have unfinished business to take care of before leaving the physical world. Instead of proceeding forward towards the light when their physical body died, these spirits have remain trapped between the physical and the astral world and can sometimes be seen, heard or otherwise perceived by the living.

Can spirits be seen?

In the physical world, most people cannot see spirits, who inhabit other planes of existence, since there is a difference of vibrational frequency between the physical and the spiritual worlds. But there are exceptions, such as sensitives, mediums and astral travelers. What happens is that either the spirit lowers its vibrational frequency to be able to be seen by people in the physical world, or that the people in the physical world raise their vibrational frequency high enough to be able to see the spirits.

Can spirits move objects in the physical world?

Yes, they can, though it takes a lot of energy for spirits to be able to do so. Spirits that move objects in the physical world are called poltergeists. Like ghosts, poltergeists are spirits that were once like us, with a physical body, and are trapped between the physical and the astral world. When their physical body died, they did not go through the tunnel, they were not embraced by the light, nor did they meet up with their spirit guide or with angels. These are instead angry spirits that either do not realize that they are dead or refuse to abandon the physical world for some reason. Poltergeists are tied somehow to the place where they manifest phenomena, such as moving objects, turning on/off lights or electrical appliances...

Poltergeists need help from someone to proceed forward towards the light.

My family and I lived in an apartment building in Modena between 1996 and 2004 that had unusual sounds going on at night. We lived on the 6th floor and there was another floor above us, where the building's boiler was located, along with some private attic rooms for the residents. Right above my husband's and my bedroom, we often distinctly heard what sounded like very heavy furniture getting dragged across the floor in the middle of the night. At a certain point we had had enough of it and went to the building's janitor to complain, as we thought he was temporarily hosting some friends or relatives in one of the attic rooms – even though we thought it odd that they were rearranging the furniture in the middle of the night so often. Rommy declared himself innocent, said he was sure that no one went up into the attic at night. He later even put a string on the main door to see if anyone moved it to access the attic rooms at night. The next time the local priest came to our building for Easter blessings, Rommy asked him up to the attic floor. The young priest said a prayer and sprinkled holy water but the nighttime furniture-dragging sounds continued. A couple of years after moving out of the building, I bumped into Rommy, who told me that the people who had moved into our apartment also heard the noises going on at night.

*****

A more recent case of poltergeist activity is currently taking place in the house of someone I know in Modena. G lives with his family in the house that had been built by his grandfather X, who died many years ago. Since X's death, the remaining family has suffered financial difficulties, to the point that the house is about to be seized by a bank. Every time a letter arrives from the bank or

> *from lawyers regarding the house, some unexplainable events happen, such as the TV turning on by itself, lights turning off and thumps coming from the attic.*

How do spirits communicate with the living?
Spirits communicate with the living in many ways:

A. Through dreams

When we sleep, our conscious mind rests and our physical body also rests, while our soul temporarily leaves our body to interact with the spiritual world. During sleep we often meet up with our dead loved ones, though we may not remember much or anything about these encounters.

> *In 1995, I dreamt that my dead grandfather Sergio was alive. He hugged me in front of the house where he used to live. When I woke up, I thought it was strange dreaming about him hugging me. He was affectionate but he wasn't a hugging person. That morning I received a phone call from my mom informing me that my grandmother Ida was in the hospital, that she had had an operation that hadn't gone well and that she urgently had to have a second operation. The doctors had told my mom that there was a high risk that my grandmother wouldn't pull through. I immediately went to the hospital and waited in tears until my grandma came out of the operation room. She survived, though it took a long time for her to recover her strength and she lost a lucid part of herself. I think my grandfather came to me in the dream because he knew how much I loved her and he wanted to give me courage.*

> *My beloved Nonna Ida had been dead about 15 years when I had this dream about her. She was sitting next to me and she was beautiful and young (much younger than when I knew her). I was so happy to see her! I kissed her and told her "Don't ever leave me again". But then I looked at her again and it became progressively darker until I could no longer see her. I think she wanted to tell me: "When you need me, I am by your side, even though you can't see me".*

B. Through channeling

Some people are able to channel spirits, such as Esther Hicks who channels a group of non-physical entities called Abraham, or J.Z. Knight who channels Ramtha. They allow the spirits to enter their bodies and communicate, in order to transmit their wisdom and advice to the living.

C. Through sounds, words or songs

When we are in a transitional state of consciousness - such as half-sleep - spirits may knock or bang on the wall, the door or furniture in order to draw our attention. Or we may hear a bell ringing or other sounds.

> *In September 2009 my dear cat Luna was run over by a car, but I didn't find out about it for some time. It might have been the same night she died, when I still did not know what had happened, that I was awoken in the middle of the night by a sad, anguished meow. It was distinctly Luna's voice but she wasn't in the room. About ten days later a man phoned me saying he had seen the signs I had posted in the neighborhood. He explained that my*

cat had crossed the street in the dark while he was driving by, that he was sorry and that my cat had died instantly.

A month later, my family and I went to the cat shelter and brought home a kitten, Atena. That same night or the night after I was again awoken in the middle of the night by a loud meow in my room that was unmistakably Luna's voice. This time however it was a very happy sound.

I believe that Luna communicated with me from the spiritual world. The first time she wanted to communicate her sorrow and to say goodbye. The second time, she wanted me to know that she was doing fine and that she was happy that we had adopted another abandoned cat to take care of and love.

*****

My daughter Valentina has a similar story to tell. Right after her cat Melchior died, both her husband and daughter heard the cat's unique meow during the night.

*****

One early morning in May 2017, I saw with my mind's eye a young girl with blond hair tied up into curly pigtails, which led me to think about the circus. I then saw a clown and heard his words in my mind, "Who do you want to be in the circus?" I heard myself reply, "The Fortune Teller!" He then told me, "Then stop asking answers from others when you already know the answers!"

*****

My daughter and I have both been woken up at night on different occasions by the sound of someone knocking repeatedly on wood in the room.

I have heard bells ring - doorbell-type sounds and once the sound of a Tibetan singing bowl when I was meditating under an umbrella at the beach.
*****

I have also heard someone speak to me. Once I heard a male voice saying "Ledi, ledi" when I was in a half-sleep state. Afterwards I realized that it was someone with a foreign accent trying to catch my attention: "Lady, lady!"
*****

Other times I have heard numbers to play at Lotto or songs with a personal message for me.
*****

On two occasions, while sending Reiki energy long distance to two different people, I heard the song "Everything's going to be alright, everything's going to be alright"... and all did truly go well for the people involved...

D. Through touching

Spirits can lightly touch our hair, or our body, but it takes a lot of energy for a spirit to do this.

One evening in January 2018 I went into a deep meditative state and asked to communicate with my new spirit guide, as it seemed that the one I previously had had disappeared. I later fell asleep and during the night I distinctly felt a cold touch on my right arm. It felt to me like the cold, wet touch of a dog's nose. I immediately woke up and wrote this sensation so I could remember it the next morning. Then I fell asleep again and felt again the same sensation, a cold wet touch, this time on my lips. It

> *was a kiss from the spiritual world! I think this was my spirit guide telling me that he was still around though I wasn't so receptive to him at that time.*

E. Through puffs of air or breezes

> *In October 2017 I was giving Reiki energy to my husband in a closed room when I clearly felt a cool breeze on my face coming from above.*
> *****
> *My daughter Valentina told me the first time I gave her a Reiki treatment that she felt a breeze of cool air on top of her head. There too we were in a room with closed windows and door.*

F. Through smells/scents

> *My daughter, who lives in a house in which no one smokes, sometimes smells tobacco and believes that it is her husband's dead relative, who had been a chain smoker and had lived in that house until death. She told me that she once woke up in the middle of the night and smelled a strong odor of tobacco near her. She said it was indisputably the smell of a cigarette and that it lasted for a few seconds.*

G. Through visual materials

Spirits sometimes attempt to communicate with us by drawing our attention to written, visual materials - such as books, magazines, newspapers, signs, movies, TV programs... They are endeavoring to convey a message to us, so be alert when something strikes your attention.

> *This has happened to me endless times. For example, when I'm thinking of a solution to a problem that seems impossible to resolve, I often find my next course of action thanks to a visual message, which could be on the license plate of a car, on a poster, in a photograph...*
> *The important thing is to notice where your eyes linger and to always ask yourself why.*

H. Through lit candles

It's easy for spirits to cause the flame of candles to flicker or blow out, as fire vibrates at a high vibrational frequency that is similar to that of spirits.

I. Through electricity

Spirits can show us their presence by manipulating electricity, causing lights and electrical appliances to turn on and off. Like fire, electricity vibrates at a high vibrational frequency.

> *Only when I am giving Reiki treatments, my CD player sometimes stops and then starts again on its own.*

J. Through coins, feathers or other objects

Coins, feathers or other items that are *significant* to us appear on our path at particular moments of our lives, which is a way for spirits to tell us that we are not alone.

I was in the United States one summer and was allowing myself to get upset about some negative circumstances. I took a walk one morning and found a penny on the ground. I felt it was a message from my spirit guide or an angel: "Don't worry; we are with you". After a few other disheartening days, I went out again for a brief walk. I again found a penny on the street and before entering the house I noticed some things half buried, half visible on the ground. There were many – perhaps 20 in all – round opalescent glass gems and they were IDENTICAL to those I had bought many months before in Italy with the intention of making mosaics. The gems I had bought were in my studio unutilized and I received a powerful message: "You have the tools/means to create your reality but you're not using them!"

K. Through sudden thoughts of places

If you see a place in your mind that is unrelated to what you were thinking about, chances are that a spirit is trying to communicate with you.

I was preparing an elaborate lunch for my family when I suddenly "saw" the Anaheim Convention Center in California. This was where the multinational company I worked for organized the Fancy Food Show many years ago. And that was, I believe, a spirit complimenting me for my cooking!

L. By appearing visually

Spirits can appear to us, though it takes a lot of energy for them to be able to do so, as they have to lower their vibrational frequency to be able to be seen by people in the physical world. This is why spirits appear for seconds and not minutes or more...

The apparition

One late morning in November 2008 I was in the the tiny storage closet of a newly rented apartment in Modena. I was about to move into this apartment with my husband Marco and our 9-year-old son Federico, who were respectively at work and at school. So I was in the closet and - embarrassing to say - I was in an awful mood as I was trying to do my best, but the cleaning products kept falling on the shelves of this small space. I complained aloud, "Why does everything have to be so difficult?! Can't anything go right?!"

I then suddenly had the intense feeling that someone was watching me. I turned around and saw a tall middle-aged man standing right outside the closet! What I remember the most was the expression on this man's face: it was a loving mixture of "worried" (What's wrong, dear?) and "perplexed" (Why are you so angry for so little?)

Up until then I had always thought that if I had an apparition, I would have screamed or fainted. I instead said, "Ciao!" while the spirit disappeared before my eyes. And then I decided to go to my "old" house to think it out.

For a long time after, I was not sure if the apparition was: my spirit guide; an angel coming to announce that it was my time to leave Earth; an astral traveler; or a ghost haunting that apartment. After talking with my neighbor and a previous inhabitant, I ruled out that the apparition was

---

> *linked to the apartment, plus I never saw that spirit again in the subsequent four years we lived there. I later spoke to Ensitiv - Italy's number one astral traveler - about this and he said that it was highly improbable that the spirit was an out-of-body explorer. Having ruled out the other possibilities, I came to the conclusion that the spiritual being I had seen was my spirit guide.*
> *This event sparked my gradual spiritual awareness.*

Can spirits see those who are in the physical world?
Spirits can tune in to our energy and perceive how we are feeling and what we are doing, but in most cases they cannot see those who are in the physical world. If they are able to muster the energy, they can actually see us, but only for some seconds.

Are spirits always in touch with those who are in the physical world?
Your dead loved ones are not next to you every moment of your day, as it it takes a lot of energy for them to lower their vibrational frequency to interact with the physical world. They are however near you when you really need for them to be. All you have to do is ask, using focused thought combined with emotion. For other ways to contact your dead loved one, see page 146: "How can I get in touch with a loved departed one?"

REINCARNATION

What is reincarnation?
Reincarnation is when a spiritual being - a soul - enters a physical body. We are spiritual, eternal beings who decide to live many different lifetimes in the physical world. It isn't considered a punishment, but a challenge and learning experience. The physical world is an ideal school for souls because it is the densest, slowest thought-responsive environment, where we create our reality after much focused thought. Each physical lifetime is an opportunity for us to make spiritual progress.

Do we leave a part of ourselves in the spiritual world before reincarnating?
Yes, part of our individual spiritual energy remains in the spiritual world for the entire duration of our lifetime on planet Earth. We can call upon this energy to support us when we are in need of help during our physical lifetime, but we must be conscious of the helpful signs coming from the spiritual world, starting with intuition... We also leave a part of our individual spiritual energy in the spiritual world also for the benefit of the other souls within our soul group. We reunite with our spiritual energy at the end of our physical life.

Why do we reincarnate?
We decide to experience the physical world for three reasons:

    A. To learn and evolve

The physical world is the densest, slowest-vibrating plane and the slowest thought-responsive plane, which means that it takes more time and more emotion to manifest in the physical world than in the other dimensions. The physical world is thus the perfect training ground for souls. In the physical plane of existence, we experience all sorts of positive and negative events, which allow us to find out what it means to have all the different types of emotions there are – from feeling poor and hopeless to feeling amused and elated. We learn and evolve thanks to all the different types of people we encounter and to the enormous variety of circumstances and events we go through.

B. To enjoy/rejoice from our creations

There are some things that can only be done in the physical world, such as creating physical objects – a piece of furniture, a work of art, a house... - or having sex, or savoring the flavors of foods, or giving birth to our children... We are on planet Earth to co-create and enjoy the pleasures of what we manage to attract into our personal reality.

C. To assist in expanding the Universe

See page 22: "How does man contribute to the expansion of the Universe?"

Are we forced to reincarnate?

No. After physically dying, we can decide to remain in the astral plane or ascend to the plane of existence that is our vibrational match. Instead of reincarnating, we can also choose to offer spiritual guidance to someone who is physically in-body. We are blessed with the gift of free will and it's entirely up to us to decide whether to reincarnate or not... Souls are however usually happy to have the chance to reincarnate, even if it means reincarnating in difficult situations, because it gives them an opportunity to evolve rapidly.

Do we have another option besides reincarnation to evolve spiritually?

Yes, when we are in the physical world, we can evolve spiritually by consciously replacing our negative emotions with positive ones. We can also be of assistance to others and intentionally reconnect with our spiritual essence.

If we are no longer in-body, we can choose to remain in the spiritual world instead of reincarnating, in order to help someone who is in the physical plane to learn and evolve. By helping someone else, we are helping ourselves at the same time.

Do we choose our physical body when we reincarnate?

Yes, we know and agree before coming to the physical world to incarnate into a specific body (Life Project). The reason we reincarnate is to experience many ways of being, which may include having a body with disabilities and aesthetic imperfections, or good health and beauty, or a mixture of blessings and disadvantages.

However be aware that *not all* body conditions have been pre-determined before coming into the physical world. Since we are co-creators of our personal life experience, we can also attract certain events and circumstances - either desirable or undesirable - through our thoughts, words and actions as well as our focused attention to someone or something. If for example we believe we are fat and ugly, we will become fatter and uglier...

When do we reincarnate?

Before deciding to take on a new physical life challenge, spirits thoroughly examine their previous lifetime and need to fully recover from any trauma they may have caused or gone through. Souls are also free to spend the time they deem necessary in the astral world, where they can fulfill all their desires using their mind. After this regeneration process, when spirits feel ready and eager to express themselves once again in a physical body - usually two generations or 100 human years later - they can once again return to the physical plane. Souls tend to wait to incarnate into the body with the characteristics that can potentially help them to spiritually evolve, such as the choice of parents, astrological traits and the environment.

Do we choose where we reincarnate?

Yes, before coming into the physical world, spirits decide on which planet to be born in and in which area of the chosen planet. Some souls choose to reincarnate in a difficult environment, such as a land scarred by war. There is no relation between the soul's spiritual development level and the chosen place, so a highly evolved spirit may reincarnate in a shanty or in a castle. The location, as well as the choice of our parents and other pre-established elements, are specifically selected so that souls have the possibility of experiencing and learning from new situations. On planet Earth, we can choose to reincarnate in a slum in India, into a wealthy family of Beverly Hills or any other location. We need to know what it's like to suffer from hunger, what it's like to grow up in a happy and well-to-do family, what it's like to be homeless... Every situation helps us to learn and spiritually evolve. Our ultimate goal is to learn to love ourselves and others, which will lead us closer to our Creator.

When we reincarnate do we choose our parents and other family members, friends and colleagues?

Prior to accessing the physical plane, spirits pre-establish who will be their close family members based on the life lessons each soul desires learning. In many cases, we choose members of our soul group - that is, souls that have chosen to spiritually evolve with us - to be our parents, our siblings, our children, our friends or colleagues.

Can we recognize those with whom we have shared a previous life experience?

There are times when you meet someone for the first time and you feel as though you have already met this person somewhere but can't pinpoint where and when... The person looks *so familiar* to you and you feel *so close* to him/her the first instant you meet. Oftentimes, this person becomes a close friend of yours or maybe even your spouse. The reason that we have this sensation might lie in the fact that we have already met this person in one or more of our previous lifetimes. The person could indeed be a member of our own soul group. We feel puzzled because we *know* that we have not only met the person before but that there is a deep connection between us. For an instant we recognize our fellow spirit from the past and remember that we had preplanned to meet each other at some point of our current physical lifetime.

Are all souls equal?
No. Though we are each divine sparks, our individual feelings, thoughts, desires, experiences and choices have led us to become very different from one another. When souls incarnate into a physical body, each has an individual level of spiritual development.

Is my life influenced or limited by my date and place of birth (horoscope) or in any other way?
Before being born, we chose to have certain physical characteristics and live in an environment that would help us to learn and spiritually evolve. The date, time and place of our birth were also chosen by us in advance, along with the astrological traits connected to that moment. The planets and the stars though do *not* create our personal reality. It is us who are the powerful co-creators of our life experience. Therefore, our zodiac sign does not entirely correspond to our personality nor to the events of our life. The characteristics of our zodiac sign are just rough indicators of who we are and our astrological chart illustrates some basic events that we may go through, while it is our dreams, our emotions and our creative skills that mold our reality.

Do I have a pre-established goal or mission to carry out during my lifetime?
In between physical lives, we decide which are the lessons that we want to learn during our next lifetime on planet Earth. We pre-establish who our parents will be (obviously with those parents' consent) and certain

other circumstances and events that will appear in our scenario. Our life plot may include lessons that we failed to learn in previous incarnations or new challenges that we wanted to experience. The ultimate aspiration of all souls is to spiritually evolve, to become more loving, more compassionate, to pursue happiness, to elevate ourselves, to reach our highest potential, as well as to help others elevate themselves and reach their highest potential.

What is karma and does past-life karma exist?
Karma is the concept by which you reap what you sow – that is, you are rewarded or punished based on your actions. If you give love, you will receive love. If you do hateful things, you will experience hateful circumstances or events. It is true *everything* in the Universe produces an energetic vibration and our thoughts, words and actions (the *cause*) have a consequence (the *effect*). Vibrations of the same frequency attract each other (like attracts like), which means that if you are kind you will attract a person, situation or event into your *current* lifetime that is a vibrational match to kindness.

The actions you have however performed in a *previous* life experience do *not* influence your current or subsequent lives. In between lives, we - and no one else, as we are gifted with free will - may pre-establish for certain circumstances or events to appear in our next lifetime (Life Project), perhaps based on lessons that we failed to learn in our previous lives. So past-life karma exists *only* if we want to insert karmic circumstances or events into our next physical life experience.

Do we choose to experience certain crises or conflicts when we reincarnate?

We either attract events and circumstances into our personal life experience through our words, acts and focused thoughts or we decided before coming to the physical world (Life Project) to experience certain events that would help us to learn and evolve spiritually.

Why don't adults usually remember anything about their previous life/lives?

Before venturing forth into a new physical life, our conscious minds go through a purification process and we lose most or all of our memories from our previous lives. We also no longer recollect what we experienced in the spiritual world (in our life between physical lives). Our unconscious minds however retain all this information. The reason we become amnesiac is simple and logical: so we can start afresh, without being distracted by our past, and devote our attention to our current life. If we focused too much on our past, how could we pay attention to our Here-and-Now? We reincarnate to learn something new. If we kept our memories, we would probably end up repeating old behaviors rather than finding new approaches.

Glimpses though of our past lives sometimes appear to us through our dreams.

Do little children remember something about their previous life/lives?

Young children tend to remember some circumstances of their previous physical life and their spiritual life. Most however are unable to communicate this information to others. Children who do manage to

179

usually find the others unreceptive. Children's comments of their previous lives and other knowledge are usually labelled by adults as "cute" or "fictitious" but what if they were real?

Conversation with my granddaughter Eleonora when she was 4 years old.
Note that no one had ever spoken in her presence about energy.
Julie: "Where does energy come from?"
Eleonora: (in a tone as if it were obvious) "Energy comes from ourselves!"
Julie: "And what if we needed more energy?
"Where could we get it from?
Eleonora: "From the sun. Energy arrives from the sun."
Julie: "But how can we get it? The sun is up there, so far away from us."
Eleonora: "All we have to do is ask. Sun, could you please give me some energy?"

Conversation with Eleonora two years later, when she was six years old.
Julie: "Do you remember when you were four and you told me about energy?"
Eleonora: "No..."
Julie: "Well then tell me now what you think about energy. Where do you believe energy comes from?"
Eleonora: "From the hands, from the heart and from nutrition."

Do we bring something with us from our previous existence/s when we reincarnate?

When we reincarnate we do not start all over again, because our soul and our unconscious mind retain what we have learned from previous experiences. We thus reincarnate while keeping the spiritual level gained and the past lessons learned.

Sometimes those who have experienced deep traumas in previous lives continue to have physical and/or emotional scars in their next reincarnation.

> *Someone I know very well has what looks like whiplash marks on his back. One day I asked him about those and he said he didn't know but that he was sure that he had never been whipped. He told me his brother also had similar marks on his back. I asked their mother about the signs on both her sons' backs, and she said "How odd" and that she had never noticed them before.*
>
> *Though there is no proof that these marks are whiplash scars passed down from another lifetime, I believe that the two brothers did have a traumatic previous lifetime together.*

Can we reincarnate simultaneously in more than one life experience?

Some individuals live two physical lives simultaneously.

> *A 14-year-old student of mine was replying to a chat box question regarding dreams. I have known this boy for a few years and have always been*

struck by his extremely high level of intelligence and sensibility. Though so different from other kids his age, he gets along very well with his peers. He confessed to me that he was very confused because he had dreams that didn't quite seem like dreams. The boy explained to me that it was as if he was living an entirely different lifetime in which he had a wife. I asked him if there was anything to indicate that this had happened in the past, but he was quite sure that his "other life" was taking place simultaneously right now and in the very same town.

Here too there is no proof that the boy is living two simultaneous lives. All I know for sure is that this boy is truly extraordinary.

Do we continue to reincarnate forever?

We reincarnate as long as we want to and as long as there is something that we still need to learn in the physical world. When we believe ourselves ready, we can stop reincarnating and instead remain in the spiritual world.

How can I find out about my previous life/lives?

We can sometimes see parts of our previous lives in our dreams. The following methods are however used by those who want to learn more about their previous lives:

A. Past-life regression

Past-life regression is a technique used by hypnotists to help people remember parts of their previous incarnations. You are fully conscious during a past-life regression hypnosis – it's a light hypnosis. You can talk during the hypnosis session and remember everything you experienced. You don't see all of your previous lives but just certain parts. Some see these past life episodes as if they were seeing a film in which they are the protagonists – so they intensely feel emotions connected to the past life scene – while others see their past life unfold in a detached sort of way, as if they were seeing someone else's life though they know at the same time that it's really their own.

The first time I had a past-life regression experience was when I was listening to a guided meditation conducted by Brian Weiss - the reincarnation and past-life regression expert - on YouTube. I closed my eyes and while Brian Weiss was saying "Relax your feet, relax your legs..." and so on, I was thinking "This is just a relaxation method that I've done a million times. This is never going to work." After relaxing all parts of the body, Brian Weiss said to imagine yourself walking down some steps. A few moments later I thought, "Something is very wrong, because this cannot be me." I was a stout, middle-aged man wearing a short white pleated skirt and a white drape over my shoulder. On my left wrist there was a wide flat gold bracelet. Then I realized that the past-life regression was really happening and understood that I was an ancient Roman. My logical mind then got the best of me and everything vanished.
*****
Some years later, in September 2016, I went to an expert past-life regression hypnotist, Gustav Birth, who helped me to see fragments of a few previous lives. I had told Gustav that I thought I could have

been a Jew in my previous lifetime as I had had many dreams about hiding some jewelry and fleeing from my house with lots of other people. But in my dreams I had never seen what had happened next. Gustav put me into a light hypnosis so I could remember everything afterwards. With the Brian Weiss meditation I had felt like I was in the physical body of the Roman. During the entire past-life regression with Gustav Birth it instead looked like I was watching my life unfold as if I were a third person, though I knew that it was me that I was looking at. I was a young woman, a Jew, and I had gathered my precious things and put them into a bag. We walked quickly, a river of people, towards a train. The train seemed more like a vehicle to transport livestock rather than people. We were directed to Dachau. Gustav then fast forwarded me ahead in time. I saw myself on my knees cleaning the floor of a bathroom in the concentration camp. I had a faded red handkerchief on my head. I saw a Nazi man enter the bathroom. I saw his tall black boots very well. I knew that the Nazi was about to abuse me. He slapped me. I felt shame and despair. Gustav then fast forwarded me again, this time after my death, where I saw my life-between-lives (partially described on pages 27-28).

B. *Akashic records*

There is a library in the spiritual world containing scrolls or books with the history of the lives of each soul. To be able to access this library all you have to do is ask...

One night in May 2017, I went to bed with the desire of seeing myself in a previous lifetime. This was the "dream" I had:

I was in the corridor of a library with a man. I told the man that I usually woke up happy but that morning I was a little bit sad. He replied, "Fortunately we have an opportunity every day to change things. God gave us a new day to use". Shortly after, a woman librarian brought us very many books and piled them on a table in front of us. The man had asked her to bring them to me. I noticed that they were all mind, body & spirit books and I immediately saw that I had read most of them. I told the man so. He smiled and handed me a book that I had never seen before. It was an ancient book and inside it there were many big glass boxes. Each glass box had antique jewels inside and was decorated with breathtaking beauty. One by one, I gazed into each box with marvel and delight. When I arrived at the last box, I saw that all the internal sides of the box were mirrors and I saw myself reflected smiling as the me of May 2017, wearing the reading glasses I often use. "But where are the decorations?" I thought, looking carefully inside the last box. Then I saw myself. It was me, yet I was an adolescent boy from ancient Egyptian times, with a folded headcloth on my head. (I later Googled this and discovered that the headcloth was made of linen and called "nemes". The pharaohs wore it with stripes but mine was a solid natural color or maybe very light blue.) Then I looked at the man who had given me the book, who was now standing further away, near a few other people. "I saw myself!" I told him. Someone else in the group said, "Not everyone is capable of seeing".

Do I have to turn to a past-life regression hypnotist or can I find out something about my past lives on my own?

For a memorable experience, it would be best to turn to a past-life regression therapist, but make sure he/she is experienced and qualified and that he/she is also an expert in exploring the Life Between Lives, which is a profound spiritual experience.

If you want to get an idea of what happens in a past-life regression, Brian Weiss, a psychotherapist and author of many books and CDs on past-life regressions, offers a free guided past-life meditation currently available on YouTube:

https://www.youtube.com/watch?v=xTnAqDPBsoY

Is it useful to have a past-life regression?

A past-life regression helps you to realize that you are much more than your current physical self. It can also be therapeutic to recall certain situations that occurred in one of your past lives, to help you resolve otherwise unexplainable psychological disorders that you are suffering from in your current lifetime, such as anxiety, fear, addictions and depression. Those unexplainable symptoms you have may derive from traumas experienced by you in other lifetimes.

Especially useful - and truly significant - is the moment the past-life regression therapist guides you to the moment in between lives, when you come to the presence of the Council of Elders. This can be a spiritually enlightening experience.

Knowing about our past lives shouldn't become an obsession though. The reason that we don't usually remember anything about our previous lives is so we can fully concentrate on our current life without being burdened by the circumstances and events of our previous lives.

Is it dangerous to have a past-life regression?

There is no danger involved during a past-life regression guided by an experienced and qualified therapist. If you so desire, you can stop the session at any time, as the hypnotist brings you to a light hypnotic state, in which your mind remains alert and conscious.

Of what value is a soul among the countless number of souls?

Every soul is of infinite value.

PART 4
REDISCOVERING YOUR DIVINE ESSENCE

PAIN AND MISERY

If we are divine sparks, why are we imperfect?

We all originate from one Source, but because the Creator gave us the freedom of being and doing what we want, we have each individually chosen to have certain experiences and have evolved differently from each other. Our spirits and souls have thus gradually differentiated themselves from one another, based on our individual thoughts and intentions, words and actions. Each being is a complex result of a cumulation of aspirations, feelings, circumstances and events experienced from its divine origin to the current moment. Our Universe therefore offers a great variety of different ways of being - differing points of view, different ways of reacting, different desires, sometimes very far from the Creator's flow of love. Our physical lives are a struggle - or a challenge - to get back to our original divine state.

Why do we experience suffering in our lives?

We are in the physical world to learn, with the objective of spiritually evolving, also through the mistakes we make and through the negative events we experience.

The circumstances and events in our life have been invited into our personal reality by us either through our thoughts, words or deeds (like attracts like) or through our focused attention to someone or something. Part of our current personal reality is also what we established before coming into this physical plane of existence (our Life Project). Whatever the cause, our life experiences are precious learning

191

lessons so that we can ultimately acquire the qualities of an evolved soul: love, compassion, kindness, gratitude, joy...

Children are a bit different from adults, since they are less likely to attract negative events through their thoughts, words and deeds. However children can - and do - attract negative events by their focused attention to someone or something negative, such as their parents fighting or other unwanted, unhappy situations that they witness at home, at school or elsewhere.

How can a loving God allow suffering in the physical world?

All circumstances and events in our lives have been put there by our individual selves and by no one else. Our Creator has given us the gift of free will, so He will not interfere with our lives unless we specifically ask for help. At any rate, the negative events in our lives always mean that there is a lesson that we have to learn - that our soul *wants* to learn. We however have the power of changing our negative event at any time by refusing to give it our focused attention (see the *Wish Come True Technique* on page 41).

How do I know that I have moved away from the Creator and all that is good?

What emotions do you usually have? What words do you usually say? If they are negative, unkind, harsh, sad, angry... then you have moved away from the Creator and from who you truly are. Your words, your deeds and your emotions are indicators of where you're at.

What should I do if I feel that I have lost my soul?
There is always space for hope. You always have the power to stop, reflect and change your course of action. Do not allow yourself to feel defeated as by doing so, you *will* be defeated.

I feel like I am in a hopeless situation. What should I do?
The feelings of hopelessness, desperation and depression are the most dangerous ailments that we can encounter in our human experience. It's the overwhelming wretched feeling that nothing is going right and that nothing ever will. If you find yourself in this situation, you should immediately seek professional help to assist you in pinpointing what brought about this state of mind and to solve it. Hopelessness, desperation and depression often kick in when we repeatedly ignore our emotions and feelings that are telling us that we are unhappy in a relationship, in a workplace or in any other situation. Remember that you are a divine being and you have the power to change your life. There is always a way to make things better. In the immediate future - *now* - distract yourself from thinking too much about yourself by watching a funny movie, by taking a walk, listening to music, reading a book, exercising, having a cup of coffee with someone dear to you, by devoting your attention to someone else's needs, or by doing anything else that is pleasing to you.

Does evil exist?
An evil force or power - such as the opposite of the Creator - does not exist. However, when He created us

- divine energetic extensions of the Creator - He gave each of us the gift of free will.

When an individual is so disconnected from his divine origin that he focuses on hateful thoughts, says hateful words and commits hateful actions, he will end up attracting darkness (lack of light) and evil (lack of love), since like attracts like.

Can someone cast an evil spell on someone else?

Just as you can send light and love, there are some who choose to send darkness and evil. Someone can attempt to control your mind using a spell, hypnosis or another technique but it's up to you to turn you attention away from it.

I was once at the train station in Modena when a gypsy asked me for money. I just smiled at her and shook my head. She gazed back into my eyes for a few seconds and then passed on to someone else. My mother was with me at the time and asked me something, but I was unable to reply to her for a few minutes as my mind felt confused. I could hear my mom's words but it seemed as if we were on two different planets. I realized that the gypsy had tried to play with my mind, so I breathed deeply, forgave her, let it go and felt great again.

If you have a hard time getting back to your usual self, pray for guidance and ask the help of an *experienced, spiritually-elevated* healer.

What causes conflicts in the physical world and how can we avoid them?

Anything that distances us from the condition of "We Are One" is a potential cause of conflict. Therefore, racial discrimination or discrimination of any kind - including sexual, religious, disability, cultural, ideological and age discrimination - is the seed of wars in the world. Ignorance, lack of love and fear – i.e. the fear of having less, the fear of competition, the fear of change - lead to intolerance, which leads to consciously rejecting the fact that our fellow man/woman is someone exactly like us, a divine essence. The key to resolving conflicts at home, at the workplace or anywhere in the world is the same: Love. If each of us would treat our fellow man/woman as we would like to be treated - always and without exception - there would be no room for war or any other type of conflict.

Does the Devil/Satan exist?

An evil force or power does not exist. A power that is the opposite of our Creator – that is, the Devil/Satan – is an invention of Man, excogitated to have control over people. Hell too is an invention of Man that doesn't exist. That said, if you believe that the Devil/Satan exists, then it is possible for you to attract the Devil/Satan into your life experience. Remember though that they are just projections of your mind and have no power over you unless you let them become "real". While the Devil/Satan is fictitious, there are however malicious, lower vibrating entities that can try to mess with your mind.

Can I unwittingly attract evil spirits into my experience?

Evil spirits do exist. They can be ghosts "stuck" in the physical world or spirits that wander around in the astral world in search of mischief. Since vibrations of the same frequency attract each other (like attracts like), you may attract undesirable entities who could try to influence your mind. If your thoughts, words and deeds are good, loving ones, it is *rare* for you to attract evil spirits into your experience, but it is *not impossible*, since experiencing contrasts and learning from these are important steps of our lives.

Can a spirit in the astral world take possession of my body or my mind?

It is possible to attract, through your continued negative thoughts, words and deeds or through your focused attention to something that is negative, an inhabitant of the astral plane who attempts to negatively influence your thoughts. No one can physically hurt you or take possession of your body but evil spirits could attempt to manipulate your mind, instilling ugly thoughts of despair or hate. Even though these thoughts only pass through your mind, if you allow your mind to continue to focus on and elaborate these thoughts, you may end up attracting equally hateful people, events and circumstances into your life experience.

How can I protect myself from dark entities?

The best way to prevent dark entities from coming into contact with you is to keep your vibrational frequency high: to be nice to others, be joyful, grateful, caring, loving... Not only will you be a happier person, but you will make others happier too and it will be more difficult for you to run the risk of attracting hostile entities.

How can I get rid of a dark entity?

If you have somehow attracted a dark entity into your life experience:

- Direct your thoughts elsewhere. The first thing you have to do is take your mind off of it, as the more you think about it, the more the hostile spirit will remain in your experience. So distract your mind by taking a walk at the park, listening to music, gardening, cooking, reading a book, doing your favorite sport or physical exercises, watching a funny movie, doing a sudoku or a crossword puzzle...

- Remember that you are a powerful co-creator and in control of your life experience. You can make the hostile spirit go away by simply ordering it to, since you and only you are in charge of your life experience. No one can harm you *physically* for any reason. No one can harm you *mentally* unless you believe that you can be and allow yourself to be.

- Raise your vibrational frequency. By doing so, you will no longer be in the same vibrational vicinity as the dark entity.

- Send love to the hostile presence. This way you can also help the entity to move away from darkness.

- Open your heart. Let go of your negative emotions - such as anger, hate, envy, jealousy,

197

greed, unkindness - and turn your thoughts, words and deeds into positive ones.

- Hang out with clean, positive people – people who think, say and do positive things.

- Do not drink alcohol or take recreational drugs as you are less in control.

- Be extra attentive to your emotions, which will always help you to understand what's good for you and what isn't.

- Make sure your energy centers (chakras) are spinning properly - through meditation, Reiki and other practices.

- Ask your spirit guide or another spiritual protector for help. If you realize that you can't get out of this situation on your own, ask a *spiritually-elevated* healer, for example a Theta healer with experience, for help. What the healer will do is to help you get rid of the energy vampire and guide that spirit towards the light.

How can I purify an object that I think has negative energy?

If you feel uncomfortable in the presence of an object but for some reason do not want to get rid of it, there are a few ancient ways you can purify it. This may sound superstitious and it is... It is our thoughts and vibrations that shape our reality but we may hold deep-rooted beliefs and those beliefs too have the power of becoming real.

One ritual is to cover the object with salt crystals and let it be overnight, then throw out the salt the next day. Or you can place the object in the sunlight for an entire day or put it in a bowl full of fresh water. Whether you decide to use salt, sunlight or water, state your intent: "I desire for the negative energy retained in this object to be neutralized and cleansed."

How can I purify a room or house?

We are powerful co-creators that use our thoughts and intentions to mold our personal reality. So how could there be a formula for purifying a room or house that is valid for everyone? Any ritual that you consider efficient *is* efficient. What is most important is your intent and your belief.

Here are some ancient rituals used:

- light a candle, place it in the middle of the room and say a prayer;

- use the first and second Reiki symbols, if you have received Reiki level 2 attunement;

- put some salt in each corner of the room, leave it overnight and then sweep the salt away through your main front door;

- hold a rosary or the Flower of Life symbol in your hand, say your prayer and burn sacred incense. Sacred incense isn't vanilla or otherwise-scented incense. You can use sandalwood, or palo santo;

- do a smudging ritual, which involves burning specific herbs, such as white sage.

Is there a point of no return when I can no longer change my life for the better?

It's easier to change your negative thoughts, words and deeds into positive ones if you haven't been thinking, saying and doing them for a long time. It's therefore best to immediately notice your negative emotions and thoughts as soon as they appear and to make amends at once. You can however change the situation at any time - there is no point of no return - by consciously deciding to turn your negative thoughts, words and actions into positive ones and to focus your attention on the people, circumstances and events that you desire, rather than on those that you do not desire. By opening your heart, by allowing yourself to express a thought of love no matter what your situation is, you will see that you will receive a precious gift from the Universe very soon, something that will warm your heart and will prove to you without a doubt that you are not alone and that you are very much loved.

LIVING SPIRITUAL INTERMEDIARIES (Masters, healers, mediums...)

Should I trust holistic practitioners, mediums etc.?

Be wary of holistic practitioners who do not teach, even though they may possess extraordinary extrasensory powers and be in good faith. In addition, anyone who asks high amounts of money for their services, anyone who tries to isolate you from friends and family members, anyone who talks to you about the evil eye, curses and spells is not spiritually evolved - so stay clear!

What do spiritual healers do?

From the holistic point of view, people do not become ill owing to bacteria, germs, etc. - otherwise everyone would be ill and not just some - but because they have lost touch with who they really are and have repeatedly disregarded signs from their body indicating that their level of energy was sharply declining (see page 77 – "Which conditions can prevent me from being healthy?").

When we are ill, our natural energy is depleted and we may no longer know how to access the unlimited energy of the Universe that can make us feel good again. Spiritual healers, such as qualified Reiki practitioners, can help those who have lost touch with their true essence to re-establish contact with their spiritual selves, so that they can restore their innate healing power.

Spiritual healers do not replace medical doctors and medical doctors do not replace spiritual healers.

What are the most important characteristics of a spiritual healer?

Love and compassion are the prime qualities of a spiritual healer. The healer should be sympathetic and understanding but also steadfast. Healers should not sponge up the patient's energy as they risk attracting illness into their own experience. A true healer has the capacity of seeing the patient as already healed.

What does a Reiki practitioner do?

Reiki is a spiritual awakening and healing technique developed by Mikao Usui (1865-1926). *REI* means universal/divine wisdom; *KI* means life force energy (*prana* in India, *chi* in China).

A Reiki practitioner has received both the first and second level attunements from a Reiki Master. The patient remains fully dressed and preferably lies down face up, without crossing arms or legs. The practitioner asks for universal energy, receives it through his/her 7th chakra (Crown chakra) and channels it through his/her hands. Reiki can be given to every living being - children, adults, animals, plants - with any kind of symptom. Caution should however be exercised for those who have pacemakers or suffer from epilepsy or multiple sclerosis.

The therapist helps the patient to clear his/her emotional blocks and reawakens his/her innate healing power by placing the hands above each chakra, reactivating the blocked energy centers and allowing universal energy to flow within the body. The number of Reiki treatments necessary depends on how off-balance the patient is physically and emotionally.

Reiki is light and love. It has no contraindications.

> **The Reiki Principles**
> *Just for today, do not become angry.*
> *Just for today, do not worry.*
> *Be grateful.*
> *Earn your living honestly.*
> *Be kind towards all living beings.*

Who is a medium?

A medium is a person who acts as a channel between the physical and spiritual world, transmitting communications from spirits to physical living beings.

What is a séance?

A séance is an event during which a medium or sensitive helps a physical person to come into contact with a spiritual being.

Who can I contact in a séance?

You can contact any spirit in the non-physical world, if that spirit accepts to be contacted by you (the Law of Free Will applies in all parts of the Universe). The spirit that appears may however not be who you requested. In addition, the spirit may or may not be who it says it is. You therefore run the risk of inviting mischievous spirits with lower vibrating frequencies. If you do establish contact with your dead loved one, remember that one does not instantly become all-knowing nor all-loving when passing to the spiritual state.

Are séances dangerous?

It partially depends on who are the séance participants – that is, the medium/sensitive and the physical person who wants to contact a spirit. Since vibrations of the same frequency attract each other (like attracts like), the participants in the séance may attract undesirable entities who could try to manipulate or otherwise muddle the minds of the participants. Teasing or malicious spirits though may appear uninvited whether or not the séance participants are higher vibrating souls.

Are séances ethically correct?

The dead do not necessarily want to communicate with the living and if they do, they can easily communicate with you in other ways, such as through dreams (see page 163: "How do spirits communicate with the living?").

If it's proof of the afterworld that you are looking for, you can use other methods – for example, by having a self-induced out-of-body experience. If it's because you want to send a message to your dead loved one, all you need to do is to transmit your message through your focused thought and it will be received.

The dead should be left in peace. We should help our loved deceased go towards the light instead of trying to keep them forcibly close to us, "stuck" near the astral/physical planes. Also for this reason, séances are not recommended.

Do mediums oblige the dead to appear?

Spirits have the gift of free will and mediums cannot oblige them to communicate with the living. Knowledgeable mediums do not directly contact dead people - not only because departed souls may not want to communicate, but also because the departed may have energy that is undesirable for the medium to channel. The medium therefore contacts and asks assistance from a spiritual entity in the 7th plane of existence, who contacts the dead person in the astral plane. If communication is deemed beneficial to the two parties (the deceased person invited to communicate and the live person inviting communication), then the medium proceeds to channel the spirit of the deceased.

Who can heal me?
Doctors can help you to remove tumors and cavities, immobilize your bones when you fracture them, give you medicines to lower your fever or relieve your pain... It's however up to us to decide to heal – it's our spirit that has the true healing capacity. We are divine sparks with enormous power! Take a good look at yourself in the mirror and ask yourself: "Have I attracted my illness through my continued negative thoughts, words or actions *(Law of Vibrational Attraction)* or through my continued attention to a negative circumstance or event *(Law of Focused Thought Manifestation)*?" If the reply is "yes", do not panic because the good news is that you can change the situation by consciously deciding to turn your negative thoughts, words and actions into positive ones and to focus your attention on the people, circumstances and events that you desire, rather than on those that you do not desire. If you instead believe that it was a drop in energy that caused you to become ill, make sure you get rested up and that you take the time to re-establish your hierarchy of life values. By trying to do too many things all at the same time, we often end up draining ourselves of vital energy and feel that we have lost sight of Who We Really Are. By

deciding to address our true priorities first, we will bring our body and soul into balance.

To get a burst of energy and assistance if you are in a lethargic, depressed state of mind, devote time to meditation and physical exercises (from walking in the sun to your favorite sport). Reiki and other holistic treatments can also help get your self-healing power going.

Can a spiritual healer heal anyone?

A spiritual healer who approaches another person with loving, curative intent can be of great help, but will not necessarily be able to heal the person. The reasons for this are:

- the patient may subconsciously *not want* to heal because he/she doesn't want to give up the extra attention and pampering that he/she is receiving;

- the sick person may not be willing to make the necessary changes to his/her life in order for the healing process to be successful (see page 78: "What are the keys to optimal physical and mental health?");

- the person may have unconsciously decided that death or experiencing ill health is more beneficial for his/her soul rather than getting well again.

NON-PHYSICAL SPIRITUAL LEADERS AND INVISIBLE PROTECTORS

Who is Jesus?

Jesus is a divine spark, just as we all are. He incarnated on Earth not to save us but to teach that our Creator is in each one of us. He came to awaken our sleeping consciousnesses and to teach us about Love in the widest sense of the word.

Do Jesus and other spiritual leaders visit the physical world?

Yes, they do, though people don't recognize them. They come to help wherever help is needed, while fully respecting our free will. Highly advanced spiritual leaders can incarnate or give us their love and assistance from other planes of existence.

What are angels?

Angels are highly evolved spiritual beings that have never incarnated.

What is a guardian angel?

Each of us has been assigned at least one angel devoted to helping us and protecting us throughout our physical life. We call this dedicated angel our guardian angel.

Our guardian angel's intent is to guide us in making decisions that are in line with Who We Really Are. Angels occasionally intervene in accidents, saving the life of the person or people involved, if those people have something more to learn from continuing their physical life experience.

Space and time went backwards

I was in my car first in line at a red traffic light in Modena, Italy. Right in front of me, in the opposite lane, there was a bus coming in my direction and I saw a car trying to pass the bus at full speed. My mind quickly calculated the speed at which that car was going and I was ABSOLUTELY SURE that there was not enough space nor time for the car to successfully pass the bus. So the car could only crash straight into me at the incredibly high speed it was going. I turned my eyes instinctively to the right and understood that it was hopeless to do anything. There was simply not enough time nor space. And I remember thinking: "This is the end."
But something really strange happened. It seemed that both time and space "stretched out " like a rubber band. When I looked straight ahead again, the bus was further back. The car was just beginning to pass the bus and I saw the car easily overtaking the bus. My eyes widened in amazement! I was safe! The light turned green and I went straight home to my husband Marco and our son Federico, then 7 years old.

Can an angel help me to solve any problem?

Angels do not make decisions in our place, nor do they create our personal reality because we are each responsible for that. When called upon, they offer us guidance and provide emotional support.

How can I ask an angel for help?

No ritual is necessary to be able to contact an angel. Whether made aloud or in our mind, our emotion-filled request for help will be heeded and answered.

Angels communicate with us the same way other spiritual entities do - see page 163 "How do spirits communicate with the living?".

Do angels have wings?

Angels are beings of light that however may be visualized by us as having a human shape so that we feel reassured. Angels do not need wings to fly, but we might see the wings as they make it more acceptable for our minds.

What are the sparks of light that some can see?

That is the manifested energy of spirits. They can be seen as sparks or spheres of light.

On rare occasions I have noticed sparks of light. In October 2016 I took the Reiki II level course. My teacher was explaining that when we do Reiki there are spiritual entities near us that help us and guide our hands. He said that our spirit guide is always with us and that our spirit guides change during our lifetime. I was wondering meanwhile who my spirit guide was and if it was the same spirit I had seen back in 2008. Then I saw an intense spark of light right in front of me. I think that it was my spirit guide showing me its presence.

What is a spirit guide?

We each have at least one spirit guide at a time. Our spirit guides change as our spiritual needs change.

Unlike angels who have never incarnated, spirit guides have and know what it's like to live in the physical world. Spirit guides are spirits that have decided not to reincarnate for the time being and to offer guidance to someone who is physically in-body. They have already gone through what we are going through and can comfort us and help us go in the right direction. Our spirit guides do not however make decisions for us. They know about our past lives and know what are the life lessons that we set out to learn before we reincarnated, so they can be of precious help if we learn to communicate with them. The way they communicate with us is the same as with any other spiritual entity - see page 163 "How do spirits communicate with the living?".

At the end of our lifetime we will meet up with our spirit guide/s who will help us to reflect on what we have learned in that incarnation and to understand what we still need to learn.

How can we get in touch with our spirit guide?
All you have to do is ask (prayer), using focused thought combined with emotion.

If you have done this but didn't sense anything, know that spirits might be trying to communicate with you but you could be unreceptive at the moment. You might not see or hear your spirit guide but you may however notice signs, little non-fortuitous events that will make you understand that you are not alone.

If you are totally unreceptive and wish to contact your spirit guide, you could ask for help from a medium, who acts as a channel between the physical and spiritual world. Or you could empty your mind through meditation (see page 238 – "How can I meditate?"). Use the meditation technique that you prefer daily for at least 10 minutes.

When do the living block spirit guides from helping them?

Spirits cannot get through to the living when the latter are swamped by negative emotions, such as depression, fear, despair... When we find ourselves in difficult situations, we should try to keep our hearts open and endeavor to keep in close touch with the spiritual world, so that the help we seek can reach us.

Do spirit guides force their opinions on the living?

No, spirit guides give us suggestions on the next step to take but are never intrusive.

What is the Council of Elders?

This is a group of very highly evolved spirits. We meet with the Council of Elders at the end of each physical lifetime. Each Elder – also called Master – offers us precious suggestions to put to good use in our next lifetime.

Can miracles occur?

Yes, yes, yes! Miracles happen every day.

> ### The car crash
> One early Sunday morning my husband and I went to the antiques market in a nearby town, Spilamberto. Going to antiques markets was also one of my Mom's favorites but we had gone too early for her. When I got back home, I however called her to ask if she wanted me to take her there and she did so off we went. I dropped her off very

close to the market and then went looking for a parking place but at that time of day there were no parking places. I kept going up and down streets without any luck. Then I turned right to enter yet another street but the right back part of my car crashed into the abnormally tall, abnormally protruding corner of the sidewalk. My car lunged forward and the noise of metal crushing was quite staggering. I was overwhelmed with anger. I cried out to the heavens: "I am trying to do my best. Even when I attempt to do something nice for someone else, why does everything have to be so difficult?" I then added a few unrepeatable words, discovered that my car could amazingly proceed at any rate and managed to find a parking spot at the end of that very street. I got furiously out of my car to ascertain the damage. I didn't have the money to buy another used car, nor the money to make any repairs. But... there was not even a tiny scratch! Anywhere!

An aching tooth

In March 2016, when I was attempting to self-induce out-of-body experiences, I "saw" Padre Pio's face close to me two different times. I was surprised because I wasn't a devotee at the time. I had heard about him, that he was reported by some to perform miracles and that he had been proclaimed a saint by the Catholic church. In April 2016 I was again attempting an OBE, when I saw a red ribbon and was wondering if it was connecting my astral body to my physical body. Then I briefly saw Padre Pio again. This time he was further away from me so I saw his whole figure. He was wearing a brown robe like he customarily wore when in-body.

In September 2016, I had a very painful toothache, probably caused by eating a hard piece of bread. It felt like my tooth had moved. I called the dentist but he didn't have time for me that day nor the next two days. It was so painful that the night before my dentist appointment I called upon Padre Pio for help. He had appeared to me spontaneously three times so I guessed that he was my protector. He did not come but I saw another friar approach me while I was in a half-sleep state. Then I heard a "click" sound coming from my mouth and felt my tooth turn! I cancelled my dentist appointment the next morning as the pain had gone. Thank you, dear friar!

Not only saints...

Some time ago, I went through a period in which I was suffering from hives. I later discovered that this severe skin reaction was caused by eating certain foods to which I had become allergic. Anyway, one night my arms, legs and feet were covered with raised bumps. It was so itchy that I wanted to scratch my skin off. I somehow fell into a half-sleep and "saw" Marina, who was a friend with whom I met up on Saturday mornings for a cup of coffee and a chat along with a group of other women friends. Marina had however died two years earlier from cancer. Marina touched me and I immediately felt total relief – the itch instantly disappeared!

Can prayers help me obtain what I want?

Since we are gifted with free will, the spiritual world will not step in to help unless we expressly ask for help. All of our prayers – especially those in which we ask with deep emotion – are heeded and answered by the Universe, unless these desires limit the freedom or the needs of other living beings.

How should I pray?

A prayer is not a sequence of words to repeat. A prayer means sincerely, fervently asking the Universe to grant you a circumstance or event that you have not been able to attract into your personal experience. It is a special request made from our heart.

How can we co-create a better physical world?

The evolution of planet Earth depends on each one of us. Through our daily positive thoughts, words and deeds, as well as through focused thought combined with emotion, we can change our current reality and create an ideal place to live and love.

WE ARE ONE

What does "We Are One" mean?

We are all interconnected, one to another, like the yarn in woven fabric, or like a gigantic universal network of energy and light. When our spirit, a divine spark of light, enters the physical body, we identify ourselves with our body and mistakenly believe ourselves to exclusively be individuals separate from the Universe. In the physical world we are indeed individuals but at the same time our spirits are energetically connected to the Creator and to each other. The Creator is in everything and in everyone, since He is the source of life and of all that exists.

My friend Gabriella taught me how to meditate one day years ago, when I was far from being spiritually aware. She told me to sit on a chair with my back straight, to put my hands on my knees, to close my eyes and to simply think about the air going inside my nostrils and the air going outside my nostrils. The very first time I tried this method, something amazing happened after just a few minutes. In my mind's eye, I saw the Universe and I instantly realized that everyone was linked to everyone else and that I too was part of this enormous system, where there was purpose and logic and perfection in everything.

The next time I meditated I expected to experience something similar but unfortunately nothing as meaningful has ever happened to me again all the other times during meditation... When I told Gabriella about what I had seen and felt, she said that I had been given a "welcome to meditation" gift.

Do I contribute in creating the collective reality?

When we have a negative thought or emotion, we emit a corresponding vibration into the Universe that not only has negative repercussions on ourselves, but is also intercepted by others. The opposite is also true. When we have a positive thought or emotion, the corresponding vibration that we send out influences our personal reality and also influences the personal reality of others. The combined words, actions, emotions and thoughts expressed at this very moment by all the Earth's inhabitants are creating the planet's collective future reality.

Does the media contribute in creating the collective reality?

A huge percentage of the news announced by the media regards negative circumstances or events. The very fact of spreading this news causes a great number of people to focus their attention on undesired events, unwittingly contributing to propagating the same undesired events in the future.

Which special individual power can change not only my reality but also improve the life of other humans on planet Earth?

Our kindness to all living beings - without exception - is our greatest power. Being kind means saying gentle, friendly words to other living beings and helping them when you notice they are in distress. Kindness is treating all the living beings you encounter in your life as you would like to be treated yourself.

Which special collective power can change not only my reality but also improve the life of other humans on planet Earth?

By organizing meditations in which many people take part, we can direct the flow of universal energy to where it is most needed in the world. The simultaneous focused thought and love of many people could do extraordinary things. As with politics, there has to be someone who organizes events in which many people are involved. Some prayer, meditation and healing groups are already active but to get things going to a higher level, your help is needed. The more we are, the greater results we will achieve. Take the time to see which prayer or meditation groups there are in the world. If you are a "meditation loner", by all means practice meditation on your own, however focus your thought and energy on something specific, rather than a generic "peace in the world". Avoid focusing on a negative situation (e.g. war, lack of) and instead find the positive equivalent (e.g. peace, abundance) and direct your thought to that.

USING YOUR ASTRAL BODY WHEN PHYSICALLY ALIVE - OUT-OF-BODY EXPERIENCES (OBE)

What is an out-of-body experience (OBE)?
An OBE is an event in which one of your energy bodies - specifically your astral body - detaches from your physical body and is capable of exploring the astral plane of existence.

What happens when you have an out-of-body experience (OBE)?
A. Your vibrational frequency changes
When your astral body is on the verge of freeing itself from your physical body, your vibrational frequency accelerates and you may experience one or more of the following sensations:

- Hear unusual sounds like a roar, rumble, thump or buzz
- Hear a noise coming from deep down your throat and out of your mouth
- Feel body paralysis
- Feel your body jolt one or more times
- Feel your body being jolted or shaken as if by something external
- Feel intense body vibrations or tremors

B. Your astral body separates from your physical body

When your astral body separates from your physical body, you may feeling a floating, sliding, spinning or plunging/sinking sensation. The vibrations, sounds and other physical phenomena you might have experienced before this stage cease to be. You might then hear voices or bells ringing or see other inhabitants in the astral plane.

C. You are free to explore the astral plane

Your astral body is much more thought-responsive compared to your physical body. So by thinking of a certain place, you can immediately be in that place. You are free to move about and explore the astral plane any way you like. You can run, walk, climb, jump, fly...

D. Your astral body returns to your physical body

Your astral body reunites with your physical body when you simply think about your physical body. You might feel as if you were falling or sliding into your body abruptly (like sliding into a base during a baseball game) or you might - briefly - feel your body vibrating, tingling or other sensations.

> *In February 2016, my daughter Valentina wanted to participate at a theory and practice workshop conducted by Ensitiv, Italy's number one OBE expert. It was to be her birthday gift and it involved driving her to the town where this event was being held, going to a conference in the evening, spending a night in a Bed & Breakfast, then a whole day dedicated to practical attempts at self-inducing an OBE. I was happy to do this for her and I had planned to tour the town while she was at the*

workshop. Valentina however insisted for me to participate too and I finally gave in though the idea of having an OBE seemed scary to me... I now have only to thank Valentina for having insisted so much, as well as Ensitiv for organizing such wonderful events that instantly raise spiritual awareness in people.

I like to be in control of situations so when we were told to lie down while listening to his guided meditation and then to music, I told myself that I would pretend to go along with it and just relax... I was instead amazed about what unfolded.

The first session only lasted 30 minutes in all and after about the first ten minutes, in my mind's eye I could see a light yellow vapor over my body that was becoming larger and larger. Then I felt the upper part of my body suddenly vibrate intensely, as if a truck's engine had turned on. My face felt like it was shaking uncontrollably (Ensitiv later told me that the vibrations are not perceived by others and that he hadn't seen me vibrate). I put my hands to my face and sat up and the vibrations stopped. I laid back down again and fleetingly saw the yellow vapor above my body and felt the vibrations again twice, though my astral body did not go anywhere.

During the second session I again saw in my mind's eye my astral body as a light yellow vapor above my physical body, then I felt the upper part of my body vibrating very briefly.

A listening technique was used for the third and last session. I felt a cold touch on my right ear and then I began to visualize a cloud above me but I was abruptly interrupted because the woman next to me sat up, stretched out an arm and said with an angry voice *"Go somewhere else!"* After this experience, I saw a deep purple cloud above my body. I did not feel any vibrations in the third session. Afterwards, each of the 11 participants explained what they had experienced. The strange thing was that the woman next to me said she hadn't sat up nor stretched her arm nor spoken! Ensitiv too said he hadn't seen her move or say anything. I was astonished as it had seemed so real to me. It took me lots of experiences to later understand that what I had seen was an event taking place in the astral world, though the woman had no recollection of it and Ensitiv was an in-body observer at the time.

I am grateful to Ensitiv for this workshop, as since that day, I have no longer been afraid of experimenting and of the unknown. This experience got rid of all my fears in one single day, allowing me to progress spiritually.

Who should not attempt a self-induced out-of-body experience (OBE)?

- Those who are mentally unbalanced.
- Those who are in a very negative state of mind (anxious, depressed, suicidal...).
- Those who have bad thoughts and intentions, who speak unloving words and do unloving deeds.

What are the benefits of self-inducing an OBE?

An out-of-body experience is useful for a number of reasons, including:

- an OBE is a step towards spiritual awakening and evolving. You personally become aware of the fact that you are much *much* more than your physical self;

- you become increasingly aware that you are responsible for your actions. Since the astral plane of existence is more thought-responsive, you immediately experience the effect of your thoughts and intentions, so you get a better understanding of the impact that your thoughts, words and deeds have in your physical life;

- you can meet evolved entities who respond to your queries;

- it's fun to experience a less thought-resistant plane of existence, without the limits imposed by your physical body and without the limits of time and space.

Are OBEs natural?
Even though most of the times we have no memory of it when we wake up, our astral body often separates from our physical body when we sleep. It is very natural for this to be so since we are spiritual beings temporarily hosted in a physical body. We start to gain awareness of our OBEs when our consciousness begins to expand.

How can I tell if I am having an OBE or a dream?
During an OBE, your physical body is sleeping but your mind is awake. Another characteristic of an OBE is that you are in control of your movements - you are

free to move about as you please since your astral body is very thought-responsive.

> *In 1994, I dreamt that I was in a bazaar in an oriental town. I was wandering along the alleys of the bazaar looking for my mom and daughter Valentina, who was 13 years old at the time. I was worried because I knew how distracted my mom was when looking at shops and how easy it could be for her to lose sight of Valentina. I wasn't able to find them.*
>
> *The next morning, I mentioned this dream to my daughter. She said, "How strange!" and told me that she had dreamt that same night that the three of us were walking together in a bazaar. Then she and my mom lost me but that they were not worried about it and went to eat at a restaurant. After leaving the restaurant, Valentina lost sight of my mom and found herself alone in the bazaar.*
>
> *This was probably an astral experience with my mom and daughter, years before I knew what OBEs were.*

Are flying and falling dreams actually OBEs?

During sleep, your astral body often truly flies, falls, climbs, jumps... even though you might not remember the events. Dreams in which you are flying in an airplane may actually be OBEs, since it's more acceptable for your mind to believe that flying in an airplane is possible. Dreams that are abruptly ended by the feeling of falling or sliding are also usually OBEs, as you get these sensations when your astral body reunites with your physical body after out-of-body exploration.

Are lucid dreams and OBEs the same thing?

The difference between lucid dreams and OBEs is that lucid dreams are played out by the mind, while in OBEs your astral body detaches from your physical body and has a thought-responsive experience. Lucid dreams are not OBEs but dreams that we have because there is something of special importance contained within the dream that we should remember when we awake.

What are the similarities between an OBE and death?

Both during OBEs and when you die:

- *you use your astral body*

- *it's more evident that your reality is based on your thoughts, intentions, beliefs and expectations*

  The astral plane is a much more thought-responsive plane of existence than the physical world, so your thoughts, intentions, beliefs and expectations promptly mold your reality. If you focus your thought on flying, you fly.

- *there is no space-time limit*

  You are free in the astral plane to move wherever your thoughts guide you – indeed anywhere in space and time.

What does an astral body look like?

Your astral body can take on the appearance of how you see yourself – such as a younger, more handsome version of your physical body or as a globe of light. But in most cases your astral body looks exactly like your physical body.

What is the ideal way to self-induce an out-of-body experience (OBE)?

Choose a place where you won't be disturbed for an hour, though not your bedroom as that's where you are used to sleeping. Turn off your mobile phone and lie down on your back with your arms along your sides, preferably without a pillow under your head. It's best not to use a pillow since you have less chance of your mind falling accidentally asleep without one. Close your eyes and relax every part of your body, starting from your feet and ending with your head. The very fact that you desire to have an out-of-body experience – a focused thought – will assist you in having one. Use one of the OBE techniques indicated here below to facilitate the process:

- just wait for your body to fall asleep while your consciousness remains awake

- imagine yourself climbing up a ladder, up a rope, going up in an elevator, taking off in an airplane ... (up motion)

- imagine yourself diving into a pool, going down a slide, skiing or snowboarding down a slope, sledding down a hill, jumping out of a plane with a parachute... (down motion)

- imagine yourself on a swing, on a hammock, rocking chair or on a boat... (back and forth motion)

- imagine your physical body becoming heavier and heavier and your astral body rising up above your physical body (lifting motion)
- imagine yourself doing your favorite sport or gym exercises (any kind of motion)
- set an alarm every hour during the night
- put on some Hemi-Sync or 432 Hz music and just relax, listening to the music
- slowly hum the Om sound (ommmmmmmm....) until you feel a new awareness, a new state of consciousness.

When is the best time to induce an OBE?
Any time is fine, though it's not recommended trying a self-induced out-of-body experience when you're too tired, since the objective is for your physical body to relax to the point that it sleeps while your mind instead is awake and alert.

Are certain conditions necessary for me to have a successful self-induced OBE?
Your physical body certainly has to be in a very relaxed state. Prior to that, a healthy diet and positive thoughts, words and deeds are helpful - if not essential - to have a successful self-induced OBE. Some find that by doing sports or other physical exercise during the day makes it easier to self-induce an OBE, as the mind continues to have the sensation of moving when the physical body falls asleep and transmits this impulse to the astral body.

Who can I meet during out-of-body experiences (OBEs)?

Whether it's self-induced or not, when you have an out-of-body experience, your astral body finds itself in the astral plane of existence, where you can meet up with:

A. Spirits who are no longer physically alive, including your dead loved ones – relatives, friends and pets – as well as souls known in your previous lives, spirits guides, spiritual teachers, spirits who incarnated on other planets besides Earth...

B. Individuals who are still physically alive, such as those who temporarily leave their physical body during sleep or astral travelers, who intentionally do so.

The encounters you have largely depend on your vibrational state as well as on the vibrational state of the others with whom you interact.

What should I do after the first sign of vibrations preluding an OBE?

If you want to have this experience, keep calm and do nothing to stop the vibrations. Just let go and direct your attention away from your physical body. For example, imagine your astral body going to another room in your house, to the beach, to wherever you would like... Remember that you are always in control – it's your thoughts and intentions that mold your reality and in the astral plane, which is much more thought-responsive than the physical plane of existence, your thoughts and intentions produce quicker results compared to when you're in-body.

How long does it usually take to go from the vibrational state to separation from the body (OBE)?

It usually takes less than a minute.

Do I continue to use my 5 physical senses during out-of-body exploration?

You can see, hear, touch, smell and taste but it's your mind that controls these senses and they are a bit different compared to your 5 physical senses. For example, your vision may be greatly enhanced - you might see at a much wider angle than you do when in-body. But it could also be that you see as if we were in a fog or can't see at all – because it's your mind that has control. Therefore, focus your thought on seeing clearly if you want to see well. Concentrate your thought on clear hearing if you want to hear well, and so on.

Do people who are blind or have other impediments in the physical world possess all senses during an OBE?

Yes, it is possible for the physically blind to see during an out-of-body experience. Any and all physical impediments are set aside, as long as the person's mind is focused on those senses.

Do I have spiritual protection when I have an OBE?

We are blessed with the gift of free will so we have spiritual protection - from our spirit guide, an angel or other non-physical being - during an out-of-body experience only if we ask for it.

Is it safe to have an OBE?

It's safe as long as we know that it's our mind that is in control of our experience. The astral plane is much more thought-responsive than what we are used to, so if we focus our thought on being at the beach, we'll immediately be at the beach. If we focus our thought on seeing some hideous creature, we will see a hideous creature. If you find yourself in an undesirable situation, you have the faculty of changing it on the astral plane or of returning to your physical body by focusing on a body part, such as your hand or foot.

If you are mentally unbalanced, in a negative state of mind or you're a fearful sort of person, you shouldn't try to self-induce an OBE as you might attract negative, fearful situations (like attracts like). On the other hand, those who have good positive thoughts, words and deeds when in-body are more likely to have enjoyable, uplifting experiences.

What can I do if I am having a negative experience during an OBE?

If for some reason you enter into contact with a hostile presence during an out-of-body experience, remember that you can:

- make the hostile presence go away by simply ordering it to, since you and only you are in charge of your life experience, not only in the physical world but also in the astral world. No one can harm you physically for any reason. No one can harm you mentally unless you believe that this is possible;

- send love to the hostile presence. Love is not compatible with negative energies so the hostile presence will go away;
- ask for protection from your spirit guide or another spiritual protector.

Just like the contrasts we face in the physical world, contrasts in the astral world represent occasions in which to learn and grow. At any rate, entities that we perceive as negative are usually simply attracted to our energy because they have less energy than we do, so there is nothing much to be afraid of.

Can someone else take over my physical body when I'm having an OBE?

No one can take over or possess your physical body when you're having an out-of-body experience. We do not totally abandon our physical body during an out-of-body experience. A part of our consciousness stays in our physical body during an OBE so that our body functions continue to operate.

What type of communication is used in the non-physical world?

Telepathy is the form of communication used in the spiritual world, which means that a spirit directly transmits thoughts and emotions to a recipient without using the physical senses of hearing, speaking or seeing. These thoughts and emotions are instantly impressed into the mind of the recipient, so there is no risk of being misunderstood.

Can I go backward and forward in time during an OBE?

During an out-of-body experience, you are not confined to a certain period in time. You are in fact free to explore past, present and future scenarios. The past and the future do not exist outside of the physical world - only the extended present exists in the spiritual world. Out-of-body explorers are free to go at any time to any point of time without any lapse in time. Explorers may also find upon awaking that just a few minutes have gone by in the physical world, while their OBE lasted hours or days.

Why can out-of-body explorers walk through walls?

During an OBE, your body is much less dense than physical objects, which are the densest of all, and so you can walk through doors, walls, windows and other material objects.

Is reality different during OBEs compared with in-body reality?

Yes, since the astral plane of existence is much more thought-responsive than the physical world. Therefore you can shape your reality - through your thoughts and intentions - much quicker compared to when you're in-body.

In which circumstances are spontaneous OBEs most likely to occur?

It is more frequent for children or adults to have spontaneous out-of-body experiences:

- after doing intense physical activities;

- when very ill (for example: coma, very high fever);
- when undergoing general anesthesia;
- when enduring dramatic situations (in this case, the astral body detaches from the physical body to distance itself from the trauma that is being experienced).

At what age is it most likely to have a spontaneous OBE?

Children are more likely to have spontaneous OBEs compared to adults.

Is everyone capable of self-inducing an OBE?

Yes, anyone who desires having an out-of-body experience is potentially capable of having one. Whether or not you successfully self-induce an OBE though depends on a number of factors, starting with your ability to relax all parts of the physical body.

If you are on a path of spiritual growth, evolved entities may help you to have an out-of-body experience.

How do I perceive physical objects during an OBE?

A distinction must be made here between having an OBE in the physical world and having an OBE in the astral plane. If you are using your astral body in the physical world, your hand/body will pass through the physical object because your astral body is less dense than the physical object. If you instead are using your astral body in the astral plane, you perceive the objects as solid since your body has the same density.

Can I move a physical object during an OBE?

No, because your astral body is less dense than physical objects.

Can I be seen or heard by a physical in-body person when I am out-of-body?

Yes, an out-of-body explorer can conceivably be seen or heard by a physical in-body person however only if that person is a sensitive or has a high vibrational frequency at that moment. Specific research should be made in this field.

> *I was in an airplane that was approaching an airport. I could distinctly see every detail of the landing process: I could see the buildings of the city gradually coming closer, I could see the sky, the interior of the airplane and myself sitting on the right side of the plane next to a window. I felt as if I had 360° super-vision.*
>
> *At the same time, I was aware that my body was lying in bed next to my husband who was fast asleep. I wanted to wake him and tell him about what I was experiencing and I tried to, but I soon discovered that it was impossible to communicate with him. So I decided to focus entirely on and enjoy my out-of-body experience and for a short while I continued to see the landing process but my vision suddenly blurred and then I was only in my bed.*

How can I return to my body during an OBE?

Just think of your physical body and you will return to it. Some astral experts suggest thinking of a particular part of your body, such as your big toe.

I have tried for months to self-induce an OBE without success. What should I do?

Make sure that you first deeply relax all parts of your body. You should have the impression that your body is sleeping, while your mind is alert. You can tell that you are in this state because you can hear your physical body breathing differently than when awake – your breathing slows down and becomes more regular. A healthy frugal diet as well as positive thoughts, words and deeds when in-body are also essential for a successful out-of-body experience.

EVOLVING SPIRITUALLY

Why are there many religions?
Religions have been created by man with the intention of bringing us closer to the Creator. The different types of religions are simply different paths leading to the same objective. There is no religion that holds the absolute truth since it's man and not the Creator who has established the rules and regulations to abide by. Beware however of so-called religions that limit personal freedom and that promote hate or prejudice.

Do I need to pray in a church, temple, mosque...?
The Creator is an omniscient (all knowing), overwhelmingly powerful source of energy and pure unconditional love. He is omnipresent – that is, present everywhere at the same time. So we do not need to go into a certain building to be able to communicate with our Creator. But if it makes you feel better to go into a church, a temple or a mosque, by all means do so.

What is spirituality?
Spirituality does not mean reciting a series of words that you have memorized. Spirituality is the state of connecting to your higher self, the non-physical part of you that is an extension of the Creator.

Can one be deeply religious but lacking in spirituality?
Unfortunately so. There are people who are religious, in the sense that they assiduously practice their faith, who repeat prayers daily and donate money to their place of cult, but who are not spiritual since they do

not love their fellow men owing to racial, class, gender, religious or other types of discrimination.

Should I simply believe what I am told, what I read etc.?

Definitely not. It is up to each one of us to find where the truth lies, so do not passively accept dogmas or opinions expressed by others, since you are a divine spark with the intelligence of coming to your own conclusions. By exploring, experimenting, thinking and feeling, you can find the way to connect to your spiritual essence and to the Creator.

Is materialism harmful to my spiritual growth?

Excessive attachment to materialistic things that do not fit into the category of "basic needs" (air, water, food, shelter, clothing, education and good personal relationships), prevent us from evolving spiritually. We are in the physical world also to enjoy material pleasures but there should be a balance between physical and spiritual – not too much of one nor the other.

Which techniques can help me to grow spiritually?

Here are some of the many options at your fingertips:

1. *Learn to actively transform a negative emotion or thought into a positive one*:
   a. Recognize that you are having a negative emotion or thought;
   b. Never express your negative emotions or thoughts in words (aloud) or in deeds (slamming door etc.);

c. Observe your negative emotion or thought objectively, neutrally, as if you were not involved;
d. Open your heart;
e. Be grateful for what you are and what you have.

If you are unable to transform your negative emotion or thought into a positive one, then distract your mind by taking a walk, listening to music, reading a book, exercising, watching a funny movie...

2. *Meditation*

Meditation is a technique used to quiet your mind, so that your physical self can connect to your spiritual self (your soul) and to the Creator. It also helps you to relax and heal emotionally and physically. See page 238: "How can I meditate?"

3. *Hatha Yoga*

This is a meditative practice that combines a sequence of body movements with breathing exercises.

4. *Self-induced out-of-body experience* (see pages 218-234 "USING YOUR ASTRAL BODY WHEN PHYSICALLY ALIVE - OUT-OF-BODY EXPERIENCES (OBE)")

5. *Reiki* (pronounced ray-key)

Reiki is a spiritual awakening and healing technique. Reiki is not something you can learn from a book. It has to be transmitted to you by a Reiki Master.

6. *Qigong* (pronounced chee-gong)

This is an ancient Chinese mind-body-spirit technique that involves doing gentle physical movements combined with controlled breathing and meditation. It helps you unblock your *chi*, the vital energy in your body, so that your body has the energy required to restore good health.

7. *Tai Chi*

Tai Chi is an ancient Chinese martial art designed for self-defense. It is performed by making slow-moving, harmonious exercises along with meditation and breathing exercises. Tai chi optimizes the flow of vital energy in the body, thereby promoting physical and mental well-being.

Other techniques include *ThetaHealing®*, *past-life regression hypnosis*, *family constellations*, *ashtanga yoga*, *kriya yoga* and more...

Which is the best of the above techniques?

You have to experiment and find out which is the best technique for you. At any rate, be very picky as to who your teacher is, because there are real Masters who teach holistic techniques and there are those who are entirely lacking in spirituality. Remember though that you are the true Master of yourself.

How can I meditate?

There are many ways to meditate. Here are a few... Turn off or mute your mobile phone and choose a place where you won't be disturbed. Lie down or sit with your back straight. If you decide to sit, put your hands on your knees and your feet on the ground. Do not cross your legs. Choose one of the following meditation techniques and perform for about 15-20 minutes, possibly every day:

- Close your eyes and focus your attention on a sound, such as the sound of a spinning fan, a dripping faucet, the inner sound coming from our ears, the sound of waves on the beach or meditation music. The sound should be monotonous and repetitive.

- With your eyes open, focus your attention on a lit candle, the stars, the sunset, a tree...

- Close your eyes and repeat a mantra, which is an inspiring word or phrase of your choice. Examples are "I am that I am", which means that the Creator is within you, "I am One", or my favorite: "I shall shine like a star!"

- Close your eyes and focus on breathing through your nose. Think, as you inhale, of the air entering your nostrils and think, as you exhale, of the air exiting your nostrils.

If you find your mind wandering while you're meditating (such as thinking about the office work you need to do), gently direct your mind to return to the chosen point of focus.

What can hinder my spiritual growth and prevent me from creating the reality I desire?

- All negative thoughts, emotions, words and deeds hinder our spiritual growth and prevent us from creating the reality we desire. It's the choices that we make daily that either let us advance along the path to happiness or lead us into the darkest of alleys.

- An excessive physical or psychological attachment to any physical object, person or place slows down spiritual growth.

- The force of habit and fear of all that is new can prevent us from evolving spiritually as we do not do what we *really* want – we limit ourselves from being and doing or having what we *really* want and instead do what we are *accustomed* to do.

- Not making good use of our time - such as spending *a lot* of time on social networks or watching tv, to the point that our mind is "on standby" - hinders our spiritual growth.

- A lazy mind and a lazy body are our own worst enemies, hindering ourselves from reaching our full potential.

- Focusing on the lack of what we desire (lack of money, lack of a romantic relationship, lack of good health...) prevents us from being vibrationally in sync with what we desire, therefore preventing us from getting what we desire.

- When we focus more on the past (nostalgia) rather than on the present moment we are also slowing down our spiritual growth.

When am I ready to have mystical experiences?

Mystical experiences can happen to you at any point of your life. These experiences occur because there is something that you need to learn from them at that moment of your life.

You will begin though to have more and more mystical experiences only when your thoughts, words and deeds are positive most of the time. A loving, healthy lifestyle and an open mind are the gateways to uplifting mystical experiences.

I have awakened and am evolving spiritually. What is the next step?

The next step of those who have awakened - that is, those who have discovered that they are much more than their physical body – is to endeavor to understand more... more about the universal laws, more about how to transform their personal reality, and how to get closer to the Creator. And there is no end to learning and evolving.

Many also deeply desire to help others to awaken too. The problem is that not everyone you know is ready nor willing to listen to you... You can teach, heal and be an example of love, balance and harmony, but acceptance of what you have learned is up to each individual. If others seem interested in listening to you, you can tell them that there is a more joyful, happier way to live life if they would just open their hearts, notice their emotions and be daily conscious of the words they say and the actions they take.

Are there any physical effects of a spiritual awakening?

You may feel pressure at the top of your head (7th chakra) or between your eyebrows (6th chakra), or a tingling sensation in your head. This means you are opening up to the divine. And/or you may feel a tingling sensation in your body, as if you had drunk 20 cups of coffee. This indicates that you are vibrating at

a higher frequency than before. Other physical effects
may include:

- trouble sleeping, owing to your altered level of
  energy;
- dizziness, due to shifting energy;
- buzzing, ringing sounds in the ear or hearing
  high-pitched frequencies could indicate that you
  are opening up to receive the gift of
  clairaudience, which means the ability of hearing
  communications from the spiritual world - either
  in your mind (internally) or in your physical ears
  (externally);
- feeling strong energy in your hands.

Which are the spiritual guidelines of a life on planet Earth?

Love yourself and acknowledge your divine essence,
which makes you a powerful co-creator of your life
experience. Learn to love others, even though they
may be very different from you and not hold your
same views. (See page 112: "How can I learn to love
others?")

How is the best way to raise my child?

*A. Make sure your vibrational frequency is high
and that your heart is open*

By tending to the way we feel, by being very careful
about our emotions and endeavoring to feel good, we
are transmitting vibrations that are beneficial to our
child. It doesn't matter whether the child is born yet or
not, because he/she picks up the vibrations from
parents and others in his/her vicinity and begins to co-

create his/her life experience even when in the womb. Children are like a sponge and absorb everything that they observe in their environment so we must pay extreme attention to our thoughts, feelings, words and actions in the presence of a child. Let's learn to be in control of our negative emotions, let's be an example of balance and love for our children and for all children. Let's have a ready smile, help them and others when help is needed, and do everything in our power to make them proud to have us as parents.

B. *Protect your children from people who are aggressive and violent*

Notice, notice, notice. Too many of us are not attentive enough towards our children. Is our spouse aggressive or violent? Who are our children's school teachers and how do they treat them? Then there are those parents who do notice but... are afraid of change. Sometimes something dramatic needs to be done, such as reporting abuse, asking help from a social worker, speaking to the school principal. Notice and take immediate action to protect your child.

C. *Teach them that they too are powerful co-creators of their life experience*

Help them to learn what you have learned – that it is our own thoughts and emotions that mold our personal reality, that attract and manifest all the circumstances and events in our life experience.

D. *Make sure they get a good education*

Education is a basic need. You are limiting your child's freedom if you do not help him/her to have a good education, because in our society it's more difficult to be or do or have what you want without one. A good education doesn't mean going to the most expensive schools, nor having to study day and night for 12 or more years. It doesn't mean memorizing word for word, but it does mean enriching our minds with basic notions about our world. It means learning to read, write, communicate verbally, to use our creativity and to get along with each other. It means learning compassion, learning not to judge, learning how to have an open heart and mind. If your child gets a good basic education, he/she can later decide to do anything he/she desires to do as a job; otherwise, his/her job possibilities are limited.

E. Allow them to reach their full potential
Do not smother your children's ambitions nor limit their freedom by making them conform to your ideas or those of others, but let them explore and learn and find their own path to happiness.

What should parents do if their children have so-called paranormal abilities?
Parents should help their children realize that paranormal abilities are actually natural, innate abilities that we all have, except that some people have more developed gifts than others. If they for example see things that others do not see, reassure the children that they are not going crazy, that all is well... Many parents minimize or ignore what their children tell them, as paranormal abilities are considered a taboo in many societies. Vice versa, do not jump to conclusions as soon as your child tells you something that appears to be paranormal, but listen to your child and find out more on the subject.

What is enlightenment?
Enlightenment is discovering that this moment is simply perfect. Enlightenment means to be truly and

wholly conscious of our divine nature. The path to enlightenment is to heed our emotions, to let go of fear, to let go of the past, to let go of habit, to let go of attachment to any physical person, place or object, to let go... and to simply *love and be*.

What makes a successful life?

Success isn't measured by how much money or how many objects you've accumulated but by the amount of joy you have experienced and by the amount of joy you have brought to others during your lifetime.

How do you feel when in you are in tune with who you really are?

Your heart is open, you feel enthusiastic, full of energy and you notice all the beauty that surrounds you. It's amazing how different the world appears to you when you are in tune with who you really are. When you are aligned with your spiritual self, you *know* that there is nothing that you couldn't do, including miracles.

What is something good to keep in mind every night?

You are an eternal being with a limited amount of time to experience the physical world. Ask yourself every night before sleep: "What do I want? What do I want to do? How do I want to interact with others?" Plan your tomorrow. Imagine in your mind's eye the way you want your tomorrow to be like. Be thankful. Those who don't plan, who let themselves passively go with the tide, are at the mercy of anyone or anything coming their way through their unconscious thoughts and emotions.

Do not waste your precious time. Do not put off being happy or kind to others. Life is not some vague moment in the future, so find a way to be joyful and loving *now*.

How should I start my day?
When you awake, joyfully remind yourself that you are a divine, powerful co-creator and that your mission is to be happy and kind to others. Remember your other intents for the day, keep your priorities and desires in mind and do not let yourself be deviated from your path. If you have important meetings planned for the day, decide in advance how you want things to go.

> *I used to travel often for business and so I had to stay in hotels around the world. In one hotel in the U.S., my wakeup call was a recorded message saying: "Today is the first day of the rest of your life". At the time, I thought it was kind of corny, but now that I'm older and wiser ;-) , I know that each day can be a fresh new beginning if you want.*

How can I live a life of value?
You are the architect of your life and have the power - through your positive thoughts, words and actions, as well as through your focused thoughts combined with emotion - to reach your full potential in this lifetime. Dance to your own music, follow your dreams and allow others to do the same. Dare to be great, dare to be happy!

BIBLIOGRAPHY & FURTHER READING

Rosemary Altea: "Proud Spirit"; "You Own the Power"; "The Eagle and the Rose"

Salvatore Brizzi: "Risveglio"; "Officina Alkemica" *(Not yet translated into English)*

Silvia Browne and **Lindsay Harrison**: "The Other Side and Back: a Psychic's Guide to Our World and Beyond"

William Buhlman: "The Secret of the Soul – Using Out-of-Body Experiences to Understand Our True Nature"; "Adventures Beyond the Body. How to experience out-of-body travel"; "Adventures in the Afterlife"

Dalai Lama: "The Art of Happiness"

Laura Day: "How to Rule the World from your Couch"; "Practical Intuition"; "The Circle – How the power of a single wish can change your life"; "Welcome to Your Crisis"

Virginio De Maio: "Filmatrix – Cambia la tua vita grazie al potere nascosto nei film" *(Not yet translated into English)*

René Egli: "The LOL^{2}A-Principle: The Perfectness of the World"

Ensitiv: "Nella Mente di un Defunto"; "Viaggiatore Astrale"; "Manuale per Sopravvivere Dopo la Morte" *(Not yet translated into English)*

Mark Fisher: "The Instant Millionaire"

Thich Nhat Hanh: "Peace is Every Step"

Esther and Jerry Hicks: "Ask and it is Given"; "The Amazing Power of Deliberate Intent/Living the Art of Allowing"; "The Law of Attraction"; "Getting into the

Vortex"; "Money and the Law of Attraction"; "The Astonishing Power of Emotions"

Napoleon Hill: "Think and Grow Rich"

John Holland and **Cindy Pearlman**: "Born knowing – A medium's journey accepting and embracing the spiritual gifts"

Melissa Joy Jonsson: "M-Joy Practically Speaking – Matrix Energetics and Living Your Infinite Potential"

J.Z. Knight: "Ramtha – The White Book"

Elisabeth Kübler-Ross: "The Wheel of Life"

Robert A. Monroe: "Journeys Out of the Body"; "Far Journeys"

Raymond Moody Jr and Paul Perry: "Paranormal. My Life in Pursuit of the Afterlife"; "Life After Life"

Joseph Murphy - "The Power of Your Subconscious Mind"

Michael Newton: "Journey of Souls"

Jane Roberts: "Seth Speaks"; "How to Develop your ESP Power"; "The Magical Approach"

Rebecca Rosen with **Samantha Rose** – "Spirited"; "Awaken the Spirit Within"

Florence Scovel Shinn – "The Game of Life and How to Play It"; "The Power of the Spoken Word"

Igor Sibaldi – "Il Mondo dei Desideri" *(Not yet translated into English)*

Eckhart Tolle – "Practising the Power of Now"

Andy Tomlinson: "Exploring the Eternal Soul"

Brian Weiss: "Through Time into Healing", "Many Lives, Many Masters"

Stuart Wilde: "Miracles"

Paramahansa Yogananda – "Autobiography of a Yogi"; "How to Awaken Your True Potential"

ABOUT THE AUTHOR

When I was in my early teens I told my little brother: "I can see energy!" He laughed and replied, "Julie, you need a microscope to do that!" I actually thought I could but after that I kept this information for myself. The years went by and every so often I was able to foresee events that were about to happen: my pets dying (one for unknown reasons, another run over by a car), numbers appearing in black on the wall of a casino in Venice (that turned out in just the right sequence at the roulette table near me), just to name a few... I often wondered about how I was able to predict such events. The people I talked about it to always said that it was simply a coincidence. At a certain point I was amazed by all the coincidences coming my way but couldn't figure out the hows and whys.

I was a complete atheist at the time. If a book had the word "God" in it, I would immediately decide that the book was no longer interesting and abandoned it, because the word denoted for me a relation to religious dogmas that I felt were not mine.

Everything began to gradually change for me when two extremely startling events happened to me. (See page 208 "Space and time went backwards" and page 170 "The apparition").

Some time later, near Christmas time, I happened to go inside a little book shop that also sold used books. I was looking around for some gifts and noticed a section dedicated to How-To books, such as how to rule the world from your couch and books on how to get rich, happy, thin... fast by using the guarded secrets

– now revealed – used by ancient celebrities, including Plato, Galileo, Edison, Einstein... Fantastic! I wanted to find out more and became a frequent client at that bookshop. And the great thing about it was that the word "God" was never - or hardly ever - mentioned in any of those books so I read them from start to finish.

That was just the beginning, because from then on my mind and soul hungered to know more. More about reincarnation, about our lives between reincarnations, about spirit guides, about astral travel. And especially about the nature of the Universe, about quantic energy, the Law of Vibrational Attraction and the incredible powers we have if we respect certain criteria. And all that - along with all my personal experiences - has led me to *know* that the Creator indeed exists and that there is a logic to our Universe. It's not chaos and coincidence...but order and meaning in everything.

With my spiritual awakening, I developed more clairvoyant (clear seeing) and clairaudient (clear hearing) abilities. Or rather, I became progressively more open to interpreting what spirits were trying to communicate to me.

And yes, I confirm that I can indeed see energy! Especially on sunny days and when I channel Reiki energy.

During my past-life regression hypnosis session in September 2016, I was brought to the presence of the Council of Elders at the end of my previous physical lifetime. The second Elder that approached me gave me a scroll of paper symbolizing the future that was mine to write and decide. The same spiritual being had a gold scepter in his hand that was used to heal others. He placed the scepter on the top of my head and I could feel energy flow into my entire body.

At the end of the session, after other Elders had given other precious advice, the hypnotist told me to test whether my hands had a healing effect on myself, for example to put my hands on my head the next time I had a headache. I didn't think much about this – in the sense that I heard what he said but the meaning didn't sink in... Anyway, just a week later I went to a first level Reiki course conducted by Massimo Ballestrazzi without really knowing what Reiki was. There I discovered about the possibility of channeling Universal Energy and activating the Hands of Light for the purpose of helping myself and others to raise their vibrations and awaken the power of self-healing. After talking about the notions, we created a sphere of energy which I saw! I saw Massimo hand over a globe of light to another course participant who was wearing black clothes so I could distinctly see this sphere of energy. Afterwards, the Reiki Master performed an individual initiation on each single participant – there were just three of us. When it was my turn, I closed my eyes but I sensed that he put his hands above my head. I instantly felt a very strong flow of energy, to the point that my eyes went into REM state. I was so amazed that I kept repeating, "Wow! Wow! Wow!" I could SEE the energy and FEEL the energy. It was so beautiful!

After this wonderful experience, I started doing Reiki to myself, then proceeded on to the second Reiki level and began helping others. For almost two years I did not ONCE have a headache, a sore throat, the flu... anything at all... Because every *time I noticed that my energy level had dropped - I had talked or done too much that day or had done things that were not in harmony with what I really wanted to be or do - I gave myself Universal Energy and woke up feeling perfectly well. You have to notice the signs your body is conveying to you and do what is necessary to reinstate your well-being, whether it's by using Reiki, yoga or other methods to help the energy to flow, or by changing something within your life.*

SIGNIFICANT QUOTES, POEMS & SONGS

Nikola Tesla (1856-1943): *"If you want to find the secrets of the universe, think in terms of energy, frequency and vibration."*

? Enzo Ferrari (1898-1988) **or Walt Disney** (1901-1966):*"If you can dream it, you can do it."*

Giordano Bruno (1548-1600): *"Whether we like it or not, we are the cause of ourselves. When we are born in this world, we fall into the illusion of the senses: we believe in what appears. We do not know that we are blind and deaf. So we are gripped with fear and forget that we are divine and that we can change the course of events (...)."*

Song by Cat Stevens – now known as Yusuf Islam (1948-alive)
IF YOU WANT TO SING OUT, SING OUT
"Well, if you want to sing out, sing out
And if you want to be free, be free
'Cause there's a million things to be
You know that there are
And if you want to live high, live high
And if you want to live low, live low
'Cause there's a million ways to go
You know that there are
You can do what you want
The opportunity's on
And if you can find a new way
You can do it today
You can make it all true

And you can make it undo
You see, ah ah ah
It's easy, ah ah ah
You only need to know
Well, if you want to say yes, say yes
And if you want to say no, say no
'Cause there's a million ways to go
You know that there are
And if you want to be me, be me
And if you want to be you, be you
'Cause there's a million things to do
You know that there are (...)".

Bashar channeled by Darryl Anka: *"Everything is energy and that's all there is to it. Match the frequency of the reality you want and you cannot help but get into that reality. It can be no other way. This is not philosophy, this is physics."*

Song from the musical "The Sound of Music" – lyrics by Oscar Hammerstein II:
"Climb every mountain
Search high and low
Follow every byway
Every path you know.
Climb every mountain
Ford every stream
Follow every rainbow
'Till you find your dream.
A dream that will need
All the love you can give
Every day of your life
For as long as you live.
Climb every mountain
Ford every stream

Follow every rainbow
'Till you find your dream."

Abraham channeled by Esther Hicks: *"Let your alignment be first and foremost, and let everything else be secondary. And not only will you have an eternally joyous journey, but everything you have ever imagined will flow effortlessly into your experience. There is nothing you cannot be or do or have—but your dominant intent is to be joyful. The doing and the having will come into alignment once you get that one down."*
and
"Life is supposed to be fun!"

Giuseppe Ungaretti (1888-1970): *"M'illumino d'immenso."* (I enlighten myself with immensity)

Song from Walt Disney's Cinderella – lyrics by Al Hoffman, Jerry Livingston, Mack David:
"A dream is a wish your heart makes
When you're fast asleep.
In dreams you will lose your heartache.
Whatever you wish for, you keep.
Have faith in your dreams and someday
Your rainbow will come smiling through.
No matter how your heart is grieving,
If you keep on believing,
The dream that you wish will come true.
A dream is a wish your heart makes
When you're feeling small.
Alone in the night you whisper,
Thinking no one can hear you at all.
You wake up with the morning sunlight
To find fortune that is smiling on you.
Don't let your heart be filled with sorrow

For all you know tomorrow,
The dream that you wish will come true."

Ensitiv (19??-alive):
"Sleep if you want to awaken!"
and
"Everyone of us has a revolutionary tool in our homes, a
weapon that could change our lives and make us less
slaves and victims of castes that do not wish for the
evolution of the human species. By using this tool we will
be able to fight the economic crisis, terrorism, the
systematic destruction of the environment and of the
individual... An object so revolutionary as to frighten
lobbies and religions, politicians and instigators... You
just have to learn how to use it properly. Approach your
TV and turn it off. No protest, strike or dissent will ever
have the same power as this simple gesture".

Babaji: *"Love and serve all humanity. Help everyone.*
Be happy, be courteous. Be a dynamo of irrepressible
joy. Recognize God and goodness in every face. There is
no saint without a past and no sinner without a future.
Praise everyone. If you cannot praise someone, let them
out of your life.
Be original, be inventive. Be courageous. Take courage
again and again. Do not imitate, be strong, be upright.
Do not lean on the crutches of others. Think with your
own head. Be yourself. All perfection and every divine
virtue are hidden within you. Reveal them to the world.
Wisdom, too, is already within you. Let it shine forth. Let
the Lord's grace make you free. Let your life be that of
the rose. In silence, it speaks the language of fragrance."

My deepest gratitude goes to...

∞ ***my spirit guide***, *who inspired me to write this book and who I know is always by my side, even though I am not always receptive.*

∞ ***my daughter Valentina Galullo***, *who has supported me throughout the writing of this book, giving me her precious suggestions.*

∞ ***my husband Marco Reggiani*** *for his loving presence and for having corrected the Italian version.*

∞ ***my Reiki teacher Massimo Ballestrazzi*** *for his expert advice and his teachings.*
https://it-it.facebook.com/anellodilucemodena/

∞ ***astral travel expert Ensitiv*** *for his teachings and for giving me permission to insert his technique to wake coma patients.*
http://ensitiv.blogspot.com
https://it-it.facebook.com/Ensitiv.Sensitivo/

∞ ***Paola Del Vecchio*** *for having decided to open "Borgo Shanti", a spiritual center in Modena, where I have learned a lot (and continue to learn) and have met others with my same interests.* https://www.facebook.com/Borgo-Shanti-1125394630808516/

If you have found this book to be useful,
please help the author to promote it by leaving a
positive - even brief - review at

www.amazon.com

A heartfelt thanks!

Printed in Great Britain
by Amazon